VERBIVORE

VERBIVORE

Christine Brooke-Rose

CARCANET

First published in 1990 by
Carcanet Press Limited
208-212 Corn Exchange Buildings
Manchester M4 3BQ

Copyright © 1990 Christine Brooke-Rose
All rights reserved

British Library Cataloguing in Publication Data

Brooke-Rose, Christine
Verbivore.
I. Title
823'.914 [F]

ISBN 0-85635-853-3

The publisher acknowledges financial assistance from the
Arts Council of Great Britain

Typeset in 10½ pt Bembo by Bryan Williamson, Darwen
Printed in England by SRP Ltd, Exeter

VERBIVORE

1

On the first day of Verbivore I was wordprocessing a difficult farewell letter to my wife and listening to the radio when it suddenly went phut. But this often happened, so I just waited patiently, erasing and retyping sentences and whole paras. It was only later that.

When Verbivore began I was watching the last instalment, well, not *the* last I mean but it came to be the last instalment of.

What was I doing when Logfag began? Why I was calling Jimmy, he's in Zambia you see, and as I got through I realised I had the telly on but then.

I can't remember the beginning of Verbivore. It seems quite.

I can't remember, I was coming-to after having me womb out.

So, imaginably, hundreds of the new desperate screen-diaries must open as mimic minimemoirs, trying somehow to recapture the beginning. Or refabricate it, for it wasn't much like any of that. Hundreds? Thousands, millions. People who've never freely written down anything since school except maybe a shopping-list or a Xmas card, and even those are computerised, millions of people all over the world have turned to the written word, screened or even manuscripted, all else failing. To the disgust of writers, or wordprocessors as they now like to call themselves, who, already too numerous, do not welcome this semiliterate, semicomputerate competition, but who also, while secretly delighted by the collapse of the audiovisual, nevertheless earned at least pittances from it. As for instance:

A ROUND OF SILENCE
by Perry Hupsos
Produced by Mira Enketei
Music by Dave Letts
Stereophonics by Chet Wilson

Pre-record:	Sunday 9th March 1800-1930	Studio 6A
Rehearse:	Friday 7th March 1500-1630	Studio 4
	Saturday 8th March 1500-1630	Studio 8
	Sunday 9th March 1600-1730	Studio 8
Transmission:	Tuesday 1st April 2215	

– 1 –

1. EFFECTS: FADE IN LAST 30 SECONDS OF ELECTRONIC MUSIC.
2. *Barbara*: Ah, now we'll know –
3. *Julian*: Shsh.
4. *Barbara*: But darling it's over.
5. *Julian*: Quit cackling will you.
6. *Announcer*: You have been listening to the first broadcast performance in this country of "Variations on a Theme of Pythagoras", by the Norwegian composer Firsten Dank.
7. EFFECTS: AFTER THE WORD "VARIATIONS", NOISE OF MOTORBIKE PASSING DROWNS ANNOUNCER.
8. *Julian*: Spike those oolganiks! Did you hear what he said?
9. *Barbara*: Variations on a Theme of Paganini I think.
10. *Julian*: Barbara you bootload me.
11. *Barbara*: Debug Julian, it's your friend's talk we're waiting for not this. Nor am I all that gung-ho about deconstructed sound-effects in Augustan verse either.
12. *Julian*: Vowel-sounds not sound-effects. And she's not my friend she's my semi-redundant supervisor. I have to listen.
13. *Announcer*: This is Radio 9. The Deconstruction of Sounds in Augustan Verse. A Talk by Professor Emeritus Vivien Nicholl. Ms Nicholl.
14. EFFECTS: SEE ANNEXE FOR 5-MINUTE SAMPLE OF TALK, TO

BE RECORDED SEPARATELY, UNAFFECTED BY
FOLLOWING INTERRUPTIONS.
15. *Ms Nicholl*: Students are sometimes startled to discover that histories of the English language can devote tomes of 800 pages to the development of vowels, from Primitive Germanic to modern times, but only slim volumes to that of consonants over the same period. Consonants are the relatively stable element of language –

– 2 –

1. *Barbara*: Well, I'll go and wash up.
2. *Ms Nicholl*: – the bones. Vowels are the flesh –
3. *Barbara*: I'm going to wash up.
4. *Julian*: So? You've a machine, like everyone.
5. *Barbara*: Well hex, help me clear and carry, I'm spooled out. I'm pregnant, remember? I'll switch it on in the kitchen.
6. *Julian*: Garbage it, will you.
7. *Barbara*: (*Primly*) Message received.
8. EFFECTS: STEPS, CLATTER OF DISHES, YELL, DOOR SLAMS, MUFFLED CLATTER OF DISHES.
9. *Ms Nicholl*: – sense of historical grammar beginning with these new antiquarian interests. These forces, together with the strong classical influence –
10. EFFECTS: SIGNATURE-TUNE OF TV NEWS FROM NEXT DOOR, TOO LOUD, THEN NEWS, EXASPERATED NOISES FROM JULIAN, THEN BANGING, NEWS TURNED DOWN AFTER A MOMENT.
11. *Ms Nicholl*: – and the sonorous effect of those echoing open and close o's is much reinforced, as you no doubt heard, by –
12. *Julian*: (*Switching off*) No I did not no doubt hear.
13. EFFECTS: STEPS TO DOOR, DOOR OPENS, DISHES LOUDER, MS NICHOLL'S VOICE IN KITCHEN
14. *Ms Nicholl*: – by an apparently skilful alliteration. I say 'apparently' because the rules are in fact being

15.	Julian:	subverted. In "He threw his blood-stained sword in thunder down" the repetitions – (*Over Nicholl*) Can I help?
16.	Barbara:	But of course, Julian my love, I've just finished loading but you may switch on. And perhaps do the wooden and plastic things that have to be washed by hand? And the crystal glasses. Please.

– 3 –

1.	EFFECTS:	DISHWASHER RUMBLE, WATER. WOODEN AND PLASTIC OBJECTS CLATTERED DOWN. TALK CONTINUES AS JULIAN SINGS
2.	Ms Nicholl:	And with a withering look The war-denouncing trumpet took And blew a blast so loud and dread, Were ne'er prophetic sound so full of wo And ever and anon he beat The doubling drum with furious heat
3.	Julian:	(*Sings at the top of his voice*) Here's a wooden spoo-oon And a plastic bo-owl On a plastic wra-ack Clackety-clack-clack-clack.
4.	Barbara:	Didn't you listen after all that?
5.	Julian:	Couldn't grasp a single word.
6.	Barbara:	Oh? I understood everything. I hope I was *meant* to.
7.	Julian:	Really. In all that clatter.
8.	Barbara:	Yes, all about symbolic o's and –
9.	Julian:	Oh, oh, oh! Critical claptrap! Ninety years out of date dressed up to seem only thirty years out of date. That's all the neosubpostmodern litcritters can think up as rearguard action to defend their disappeared discipline. It's only on radio culture-hookups they're still allowed to buffer on like offline tapeworms.

10.	Barbara:	All right, I may be thunkish in your walk of life, for what it's worth these days, but I'm not in mine, and I don't make you feel you are. But if you'll bootstrap your own buffering we might perhaps be able to hear the rest of it.
11.	EFFECTS:	LAST CLATTER OF WOODEN OBJECT AS MS NICHOLL'S VOICE RETURNS.
12.	Ms Nicholl:	– rather tinny, mean effect of the front palatal vowels in *Dejected Pity at his side*, but the o's and u's are at once recalled, only to be cancelled –
13.	EFFECTS:	JETPLANE ROARS SUDDENLY OVERHEAD.
14.	Julian:	(*Yelling*) I can't stand it!
15.	EFFECTS:	SMASHING OF GLASS ON THE FLOOR.
16.	Barbara:	(*Screaming*) My crystal!
17.	EFFECTS:	STEPS. DOOR SLAMS. BARBARA'S VOICE AND MUFFLED NICHOLL-TALK AS SECOND DOOR SLAMS. STEPS DOWN STAIRS TAKEN IN THREES. GRIND OF HEAVY DOOR. SUDDEN NOISE OF STREET. HEAVY DOOR SLAMS. QUICK STEPS ON PAVEMENT WITH ANGRY MUTTERINGS.

– 4 –

1.	Julian:	I can't intake it any more. Spools, I need a drink.
2.	EFFECTS:	STEPS AND TRAFFIC NOISE CONTINUE. SUDDEN BURST INTO UPROAR OF PUB INTERIOR.
3.	Voices:	Feed-in another beer, Tom. Where's Sue? *What* did you say? etc.
4.	Julian:	Excuse me. Excuse me. Oh, sorry.
5.	Male Voice:	Oh don't mention it it's only me trousers. Hey, George –
6.	Julian:	Excuse me… Excuse me.
7.	Publican:	Yes sir?
8.	Julian:	A whisky please.
9.	Publican:	Can I have your credit-card sir?
10.	Male Voice:	Hey George it's starting, turn up the sound.
11.	Publican:	Sally turn up the sound will yer.

12.	EFFECTS:	BOXING (USE REAL RECORDING)
13.	Julian:	Oh, no! Excuse me... Excuse me.
14.	EFFECTS:	SUDDEN SWITCH TO RELATIVE QUIET OF STREET NOISE, TV VOICE FIRST MUFFLED AS PUB DOOR SWINGS SHUT, THEN FADED OUT. STEPS. WOMAN STEPS RUNNING IN DISTANCE.
15.	Barbara:	(*Distant*) Julian!
16.	EFFECTS:	WOMAN STEPS RUN NEARER. TRAFFIC NOISE BUT LOWER. STEPS STOP.
17.	Barbara:	(*Distant*) Julian! Oh, I'm sorry.
18.	Julian:	Barbara love, I'm all shot to pieces. I couldn't even stay in the pub. Boxing on telly. Come on, let's walk a bit.
19.	EFFECTS:	DOUBLE STEPS.

– 5 –

1.	Barbara:	Where?
2.	Julian:	I don't know. Somewhere quiet. Where only our steps make holes in the lamplight.
3.	Barbara:	Julian, I'm worried about you. It's only noise, everyone puts up with it. What about me in the newsroom? You just get used to it.
4.	Julian:	You mean *you* do.
5.	Barbara:	And what about the baby? What will you do when the baby arrives and yells all night? It's life, Julian, life is noisy.
6.	Julian:	Quit bugging me will you? I've got enough noise in my head without you feeding-in a screaming brat that isn't even born yet.
7.	Barbara:	(*Tearfully*) Oh Julian. You never used to –
8.	Julian:	Debug, love. There (*Tearfully*) Let's just keep walking and breathing, that's quite enough activity to be getting on with.
9.	EFFECTS:	STEPS ONLY
10.	Barbara:	(*Pause, quiet but still reproachful*) What would you do if you worked in a metal foundry?
11.	Julian:	Garbage! Only robots work in metal foundries now.

12. *Barbara*: Or piloted a helicopter?
13. *Julian*: If we must fill the silence of this side-street with verbiage let it be mine. I'll talk about a forest so still you could hear a bird-dropping drop, and a twig crack under it. I'll talk about an empty field resonant with the patter of mice's feet. We don't hear anything anymore.
14. *Barbara*: But Julian, the country's full of noises too, combine harvesters and tractors and spray-planes and milk-trucks and –
15. *Julian*: Moo.
16. EFFECTS: PAUSE IN STEPS. LOUDSPEAKER IN DISTANCE.
17. *Julian*: (*Quietly*) I'll talk about a quiet valley with a meditating stream.
18. EFFECTS: LOUDSPEAKER APPROACHES.
19. *Julian*: I'll talk about a cave whose stalactites and stalagmites increase themselves through their own stony silence.
20. EFFECTS: LOUDSPEAKER COMES UP AND DRIVES PAST QUACKING PROPAGANDA.

– 6 –

1. *Loudspeaker*: Vote your Post-Socialist candidates onto your Local Council. Thursday is Voting Day. Don't forget to vote for the Post-Socialist Candidates if you want a Fair Deal and Justice. (*Repeat as Fades*)
2. *Julian*: (*Talks louder to a yell, then down as loudspeaker fades*) I'll talk about a scrambled lunatic who can't talk to his wife in the street for the noise (*Sobs*) for the noise (*Flatly in silence left by the loudspeaker van*) I really am going bootstrap.
3. *Barbara*: Let's go in here and have a hot chocolate. It looks quiet.
4. EFFECTS: STEPS. DOOR OPENS TO MURMUR OF VOICES. SCRAPING OF CHAIRS.
5. *Girl*: Coffee?

6.	Julian:	(*Wearily*) Two hot chocolates please. Here's my card. I'm sorry love, I don't know why all this noise is getting me –
7.	EFFECTS:	HISS OF ESPRESSO STEAM. HE SHOUTS JUST AS THE STEAM STOPS SO THAT THE WORD 'GOD' CLANGS IN THE SUDDEN SILENCE
8.	Julian:	Oh, God!
9.	EFFECTS:	MURMUR STARTS AGAIN. CLINKING OF CUPS ETC. CLICK OF TOKEN IN DISC-MACHINE. WHIRR. SUDDENLY LOVESONG WAILED LOUDLY BY NASAL VOICE. RECORD HEARD THROUGHOUT NEXT DIALOGUE TOGETHER WITH HISSES OF STEAM, VOICES ETC.
10.	Julian:	Random jitters! And woman wailing for her demon lover amid a hiss of steam. (*Loudly*) Hey, can't you turn it down a bit? (*Pause*).
11.	1st Boy:	'ey Alf, 'ark at 'im.
12.	2nd Boy:	(*Slowly*) It doesn't turn down, Mister Godman.
13.	1st Boy:	That's right, you stand up to 'im Alf.
14.	Julian:	The sacred river ran.
15.	Girl:	Two hot chocolates.
16.	Julian:	At last. Do you serve peace and quiet with the chocolate?
17.	Barbara:	Julian!
18.	Girl:	The café's for everyone.
19.	1st Boy:	We're the herbitcheways anyways.
20.	EFFECTS:	RECORD STOPS.

– 7 –

1.	Julian:	Good! Silence now I hope.
2.	2nd Boy:	(*Simultaneously*) That's right. If you want peace and quiet you'll 'ave to pay for it. A token costs one pound and fifty pee. One pound fifty pee for a round of silence.
3.	EFFECTS:	LOUD LAUGHTER.
4.	Julian:	(*Slowly*) One pound fifty pence for ... a –

5.	2nd Boy:	That's right. A round of silence. D'yer want it or do I put another disc on?
6.	Girl:	Here's a token, I'll add it to the chocolates.
7.	Barbara:	Julian, don't get involved, let's go.
8.	Julian:	Okay, here's your token.
9.	2nd Boy:	Thanks Mister God-man.
10.	EFFECTS:	SILENCE. CLICK OF TOKEN IN MACHINE. WHIRR. SCRAPE OF TABLE, RATTLE OF CUPS. LOUD FLING-MUSIC BLARES OUT. CHAIR FALLS. NOISE OF FIGHT.
11.	Barbara:	(*Shouting then screaming*) Julian! Oh!
12.	EFFECTS:	CHEERS AND LAUGHTER. NOISE MUFFLED AS DOOR BANGS. QUICK STEPS. CAR ENGINE APPROACHES. SCREECH OF BRAKES. FLINGSONG BRIEFLY HEARD AS CAFÉ DOOR OPENS AND SHUTS. SCREAM. WOMAN'S RUNNING STEPS. FLINGSONG AGAIN. VOICES GROWING IN ECHO THEN ONE LAST LINE OF SONG (SEE BELOW) REPEATED OVER AND OVER THEN STOPS. VOICES FADE IN AND OUT IN COUNTERPOINT THEN SILENCE. AMBULANCE SIREN DISTANT THEN NEARER THEN LOUD THEN STOP. SAME PHRASE OF SONG REPEATED IN ECHO THEN FADE SLOWLY.
13.	Phrase:	*Lerve comes in silence* *But silence also means* *Yer lerve – is – gawn* *Silence means yer lerve – is – gawn.*
14.	Voices:	a) Is he dead? b) Just look at him, what a mess! c) Poor young man! d) He ran straight in front of me. e) What a lot of blood! f) Where's the ambulance... ambulance... ambulance...
15.	EFFECTS:	WORD 'AMBULANCE' REPEATED TO PHRASE FROM SONG BUT SONG FADES OUT FIRST. SILENCE.
16.	Decibel:	(*Small voice, almost whisper*) Hello.
17.	Julian:	(*With groan*) Hello.
18.	EFFECTS:	HIGH-PITCHED WHISTLE
19.	Decibel:	(*Very high*) Ow! You're hurting!
20.	Julian:	Me?

21. *Decibel*: No, him. The sound, it's a horrid one. Stop

– 8 –

1. EFFECTS: NOISE STOPS.
2. *Decibel*: Ah. (*More natural pitch but still very small voice*) That's better. I said, hello.
3. *Julian*: (*Wearily*) I said hello too.
4. *Decibel*: Oh sorry, I only heard *him*. Don't you want me to introduce myself?
5. *Julian*: No.
6. *Decibel*: You're Julian. I'm Decibel.
7. *Julian*: (*Flatly*) Decibel.
8. *Decibel*: Yes. Decibel.
9. *Julian*: So what?
10. *Decibel*: (*Softly*) I can help you, Julian. Ow!
11. EFFECTS: HIGH-PITCHED WHISTLE STARTS AGAIN.
12. *Decibel*: So it's *you* doing it. Please stop.
13. *Julian*: How can I? It's in my ear.
14. *Decibel*: (*Very high*) Well of course it's in your ear, it's a sound. But it makes me feel so thin (*Higher and higher*) it narrows me almost to nothing, I'll vanish soon. Oh!
15. EFFECTS: WHISTLE STOPS.
16. *Decibel*: (*Her voice veers down falsetto like a disc on power-failure*) Ugh-er! Whizz-ho for that. (*Soft normal voice*) It's unspooling. I wish you wouldn't.
17. *Julian*: You're in no state to help anyone.
18. *Decibel*: I can help you if you help yourself.
19. *Julian*: Like God.
20. *Decibel*: In a way.

– 9 –

1. *Julian*: I'm tired.
2. *Male Voice*: (*Loudly, IN ECHO*) Emergency. Emergency.
3. *Female Voice*: (*ECHO FADING IN AND OUT*) This way. Gently now. Are you next-of-kin dear? Nurse, will

		you take down the particulars.
4.	Barbara:	(*FADING IN AND OUT*) Julian Freeman, 29, yes, his age, oh, 72 Wilmington Street...
5.	Nurse:	(*IN AND OUT*) No dear, you'll have to wait out here. The doctor's just coming.
6.	Julian:	(*Softly but urgently*) Decibel where are you?
7.	Decibel:	Here Julian, I'm here. Hold on to me. Everything's going to be all right.
8.	Julian:	(*Slowly*) Everything's going to be all right. (*Suddenly*) What do you mean? What has happened? Decibel, where are you?
9.	Decibel:	Here Julian, don't make so much noise in your head, it's not the kind I like, it hurts.
10.	Julian:	(*Yelling*) It hurts! It hurts! Ow!
11.	Doctor:	Just one more second now. I'm afraid I have to hurt... There, that's over, good man. Nurse, get hold of Mr Stanton right away.
12.	EFFECTS:	FADE-OUT. FADE-IN FLINGSONG, AMBULANCE SIREN, VOICES, ALL ZOOMING IN AND OUT THEN FADE-OUT. PAUSE.
13.	Julian:	(*Whispering*) Decibel! (*Silence*) Decibel!
14.	Decibel:	(*Whispering even more softly*) Yes Julian.
15.	Julian:	(*Still whispering*) Oh there you are. (*Silence*) It's quiet, isn't it? (*Silence*) Decibel.
16.	Decibel:	(*After a pause*) Yes Julian.
17.	Julian:	Talk to me.
18.	Decibel:	(*Whispering with effort*) I... don't... exist... in silence... I can hardly... breathe... I measure... noise... you see.
19.	Julian:	No I don't see. There must be... noise... somewhere... you can live on?

– 10 –

| 1. | Decibel: | (*Slightly louder*) Yes. Oh yes. (*Weakening again*) But not in your head, Julian. I liked it ...there...I'd got used to... it... But now ...there's only... the faintest... murmur... no... not even... Oh, it's like... a tomb. |

2.	EFFECTS:	SILENCE FOR AS LONG AS FEASIBLE.
3.	Julian:	(*Very faint*) Decibel!
4.	EFFECTS:	VOICES ZOOMING IN AND OUT.
5.	Anaesthetist:	He hasn't had strong analgesics has he?
6.	Surgeon:	No, I saw we had to operate at once.
7.	Ms Nicholl:	(*Quotation which was drowned before*)

>*And longer had she sung, but with a frown*
>   *Revenge impatient rose;*
>*He threw his blood-stained sword in thunder down,*
>   *And with a withering look*
>   *The war-denouncing trumpet took,*
>   *And blew a blast so loud and dread,*
>*Were ne'er prophetic sounds so full of wo*

8.	Julian:	So that's what I missed. Thank you for repeating it, Professor Nicholl.
9.	Ms Nicholl:	As a matter of fact I didn't repeat it. You repeated it.
10.	Julian:	You mean I heard it after all?
11.	Ms Nicholl:	No, you knew it already.
12.	Julian:	How could I? It's not my period.
13.	Ms Nicholl:	In one sense, we know everything, without actualising that knowledge. In another –
14.	Julian:	We know nothing.
15.	Ms Nicholl:	Exactly.
16.	Barbara:	Why this mania for knowing things exactly?
17.	Julian:	Barbara you keep out of this.
18.	Barbara:	I can't keep out of it, I'm in it, it's up to you to keep me out.
19.	Ms Nicholl:	So you see, it doesn't terribly matter if you miss one item of knowledge in a series of similar items because providing you understand the series you already know without knowing that you know.

– 11 –

1.	Julian:	How can I understand the series without knowing the items?
2.	Decibel:	(*Squeakily*) Precisely.

3. Barbara: Why this mania for understanding precisely?
4. Julian: Barbara you keep out of this.
5. Barbara: I can't, I'm in it, it's up to you to –
6. Julian: Quit cackling. Was that you Decibel?
7. Decibel: (*Still high but less squeaky, then lowering to normal*) Yes Julian, it's so exciting, all this noise in your head, good noise this, thank you Julian, I feel so well.
8. Julian: Noise? You call this noise? We're having a serious intellectual discussion about the theory of knowledge, Professor Nicholl and I.
9. Decibel: Buzz buzz buzz. Ooh it's lovely Julian, go on.
10. Barbara: What about the baby in the newsroom? What about the baby brought by the helicopter? What will you do when the baby is born in an iron-foundry run by robots?
11. EFFECTS: PRINTING PRESS AND FOUNDRY NOISES WHICH CONTINUE DURING NEXT DIALOGUE.
12. Decibel: (*Loud*) Ooh! Macrosuper, Julian, do go on.
13. Julian: Decibel, you little traitor! Why don't you go and measure yourself in a railway shunting yard?
14. Decibel: (*Hurt*) I don't need to. Your head will do just as well.
15. EFFECTS: NOISE FADES AS MS NICHOLL QUOTES.
16. Ms Nicholl: *Yet still he kept his wild unaltered mien*
While each strained ball of sight seeked bursting
from his head.
17. Barbara: Yes do tell us about the symbolic o's again Ms Nicholl, I didn't quite grasp why they were undone, deconstructed I mean what with the dishes and the quarrelling and... the... accident.

– 12 –

1. Julian: What accident?
2. Barbara: Your accident darling.
3. EFFECTS: FLINGSONG AND AMBULANCE SIREN, LOUDER

		AND LOUDER, THEN FADE IN AND OUT.
4.	Decibel:	(*Squeals with delight*)
5.	Ms Nicholl:	(*As noise fades*) But it is important to remember that the Augustan notion of form and decorum was an ideal that in no way reflected the hurly-burly of daily life. Think for a moment of Dr Johnson striding up the Strand to the shattering clatter of horse-carriages with wooden wheels on the cobbled streets –
6.	EFFECTS:	FADE IN THESE SOUNDS AND THE NEXT AS SHE MENTIONS THEM, INCREASING VOLUME AND DROWNING HER VOICE AS DECIBEL'S GETS LOUDER AND SHRILLER.
7.	Ms Nicholl:	– with the neighing of horses and the cracking of whips and the shouting of the coachmen, the ringing of muffin-bells and the yelling of street-cries, chairs to mend, sweet lavender, knives to grind.
8.	Decibel:	(*Starting at beginning of* EFFECTS, *louder and louder, stressing o's and u's*) Oh Julian, what an a*w*ful n*o*ise is this *o*ld-fashioned n*o*ise, it's horrible, *oh* Julian don't, *oh* please g*o* back to the buses and cars and speedbikes and l*ou*dspeakers, l*ou*d l*ou*d, l*ou*d, *oh*, *oh*, *oh!*
9.	Julian:	Stop!
10.	Barbara:	Please Professor Nicholl do something!
11.	Julian:	Barbara you keep out of this.
12.	Barbara:	I can't keep out of it I'm –
13.	EFFECTS:	FLINGSONG RETURNS WITH 1ST AND 2ND BOY AS DECIBEL CONTINUES HER O'S AND AW'S.
14.	Voices:	a) I say they're yuppeting it up! b) Hey, that's Alf ain' it? c) Two hot chocolates d) Debugger off Alf. e) Oh don't mention it it's only me trousers.
15.	EFFECTS:	ROCKSONG STOPS ABRUPTLY, TOKEN DROPS IN SLOT, WHIRR THEN NEW TUNE AS BARBARA CONTINUES TO APPEAL TO MS NICHOLL.
16.	Barbara:	Please, Professor Nicholl do something.

17.	EFFECTS:	*Put another nickel in* *In the nickel ody-in,* *All I want is loving you* *And music music music...* FADE OUT SLOWLY DURING NEXT DIALOGUE.

– 13 –

1.	2nd Boy:	Jesuscrumbs! That's the wimpiest oldy I've heard in a hexuvatime. What are we into, a round of folksycountry?
2.	Julian:	It's an old circular tune.
3.	1st Boy:	(*Sniggering*) A round of silence.
4.	2nd Boy:	Say, it's Mister God-man 'isself.
5.	1st Boy:	That's right, you stand up to 'im Alf.
6.	Ms Nicholl:	The sacred river ran Through caverns measureless to man Down to a sunless sea. Here we have quite a different system of sound from that obtaining in the 18th century. The Romantics you see, knew –
7.	EFFECTS:	NOISE OF HORSE-CARRIAGES ON COBBLES DROWNS HER VOICE THEN FADES OUT. DECIBEL SQUEALS WITH PAIN BEYOND THE NOISE THEN DESCENDS INTO SUDDEN SILENCE, FOLLOWED BY HIGH-PITCHED WHISTLE.
8.	Decibel:	(*Very high*) Ow! Ooow! Stop it! Ooow!
9.	EFFECTS:	WHISTLE STOPS. SILENCE. WHISPERS. FALLING CHAIR. FADE IN MURMURING VOICES THEN IN AND OUT, LIGHT SLAPPING OF CHEEK.
10.	Nurse:	Wake up Mr Freeman, you're back. Everything's all right. But don't move your head. (*Gently but IN AND OUT*) You mustn't move your head. Don't move... your head... your head... your head.
11.	Julian:	(*Groans*) Decibel. Where are you?
12.	Nurse:	She'll be along to see you in visiting hours, dear. Three to five. But please don't move your head. (*FADING*) Don't move your head,

		there's a dear...
13.	EFFECTS:	(BOXING ZOOMS IN LOUDLY) With a right straight into the stomach, oh very low below the – That was a – no – yes, the umpire's called a foul...
14.	EFFECTS:	CROWD YELLS.
15.	*Decibel*:	(*Excitedly during commentary*) Julian, just listen to that, oh no, right, yes, go on, quick now, yes, oh, oh, oh –
16.	*Julian*:	Clamm up, all of you! And you Decibel.
17.	*Decibel*:	(*Softly in sudden silence*) Me, Julian?
18.	*Julian*:	Yes you, Decibel. I'm sorry but you'll have to go.

– 14 –

1.	*Decibel*:	(*Tearfully*) Oh Julian don't leave me, don't throw me out, I can't live without you.
2.	*Julian*:	And I can't live with you. I must have complete silence.
3.	*Decibel*:	(*Whispering*) Then I must die.
4.	*Julian*:	No blackmail. I didn't even know you till three to five visiting hours.
5.	*Decibel*:	You wouldn't... like it, Julian.
6.	*Julian*:	You mean you wouldn't. So you assume I wouldn't. (*Silence*) You seem to revel in noise. Oh you're very selective about which noises, but those you like, why, I do believe you go about creating them. (*Long silence*) Don't you? (*Silence*) You itsybitsybitch.
7.	EFFECTS:	FLINGSONG IN AND OUT. SCREECH OF BRAKES. AMBULANCE SIREN.
8.	*Julian*:	No, no (*Shouting*) It hurts. (*Normal voice*) It hurts. (*Whispering*) It hurts.
9.	*Barbara*:	(*Soothingly*) I know darling, I know. You've been very brave. Try not to move your head.
10.	*Julian*:	Where's Decibel?
11.	*Barbara*:	Yes darling I'm here.
12.	*Julian*:	Barbara you keep out of this.

13. Barbara: (*Slight gasp, pause, then effort*) Yes, dear. (*Sob*) Just keep your head still. Please. (*Breaks down*) Oh darling I do love you so. I can't live without you...
14. Nurse: Now Ms Freeman, don't go upsetting him. I think that's enough for today.
15. Barbara: (FAR OFF AND FADING) Yes I'm sorry nurse. Goodbye my love, I'll be back tomorrow.
16. Julian: (*Whispering*) Decibel? (SILENCE) Decibel!
17. EFFECTS: SILENCE THEN TINKLING NOTES LIKE RADIO SIGNAL AFTER SWITCH-OFF, REPEATING.
18. Julian: (*Still whispering*) Decibel!
19. EFFECTS: SUDDEN CUT

2

First I'd like to say two things. But you will answer my question? Mr Nwankwo am I in the habit of not answering your questions? Well – But first it is necessary to say –

Le milieu politique – – – – nombreuses *petites phrases* ce weekend qui ont fait les délices de la presse. Celle du président d'abord.

And ARE you going to call for indus – – action? I must first make it – – – your introd – –, that I –

And Dixon passes to – – – – – – – – who – – – – – – Evans to – – loses it to Grandet no, he's got it – – – oh, terrific footwork – – – passes to – – – – – – directs a header. Oh, a near – –

Having said that, the situation can't be allowed to –

For of course, libido has replaced semeiosis. And that being so, we can say –

Precisely, that is why their Chargé – – – – – – – – – – – – Office, to give an explanation and to make it plain that it mustn't happen again.

Nous avons toujours dit, nous les Commu –

We intend to seek a determined stride forward for Post-Socialism and New Democracy. But you are often accused of fudging the real issues. There will be no fudging of anything, on the contrary, we shall have utmost clarity. Clearly the general principles must be –

Certo che l'autocritica è una buona cosa, nel esercito, nella polizia, no potrebbe indebolire il corpo, puo solamente rinforzarle. E questo vale anche per la autocritica nel suo proprio partito? Ah! Non l'ho visto venire, quella! Lei fa referenzia al –

Happy Morning Hour! That's what our new morning program is called. And we can't make it without YOU. Your baby is having a first birthday? Send us a –
What prompted this new escalation? that's the question I put to our –
Entschuldigen Sie bitte, das haben wir nie gesagt. Was wir genau –
The impasse provides a certain impetus. For impotence? That's unwor –
I agree. And when a Post-Socialist Government is elected, it will be high up on the list of legislative prior –
And now that you have at last agreed to nego – – – – – – it plain that we will not negotiate. But – Not at all we must enter talks, we agree, but not neg –
I believe in lorenorder, I'm a lore-abiding person, though I can't abide lore-officers you see, bec –
The U.S. Government is very concerned about the Soviet proposal that concrete results should come out of the conference, seeing that –
We must remember the Baroque fondness for the tromploy effect and the me's on a beam –
Primo tengo que decirle dos cosas. Entonces la primera –
And will you be the candidate for the leadership? Why will you journalists – – – – – – – time enough to –
Well, birth, marriage and death and all the rest of it. What do you mean by all the rest of it, what rest is there after death? Oh sorry I didn't mean to pun. I hope not. I was merely answering your question about my themes as a wordprocessor, not talking about reality. But isn't reality –
And how long do you expect to wait for their reaction? First I must say three things –
For it's not only a question of por – – – – – violent – – – children's – – – – – attractively dressed up with spaceships and compu – – – – – – story element – – – hurling himself from a great height upon the villain and fighting – – – except that – – – like mediaeval knights. It's all as old as – – – But surely – – – deprive our children of a healthy spirit of – – – – – – what should go and what should not. I'm trying to say to viewers

– – – – – – – – – – really a problem for –
 'ere Sam, this is Dave, 'e's new, you tell 'im the – – – –
don't be so suspi – – – just surprised. Surprised at what, eh?
What d'yer mean surp –
 We can work it out quite easily, after all Christ was born between 5 and 10 BC, so –
 Oh no! not Bankrupt! Ouf! 500. I'll have an M please. No M. Your turn Dick, 8000, 750, 100, oh, no, Pass, Bad Luck! Sally. – – – – – 900. For 900 I'll have a –
 We must stop fighting last year's battles and become realistic. We must look ahead – – – – – – – – – – – – – – – But surely that isn't exactly –
 Stay tuned –
 No indeed, it isn't exactly anything, cut or uncut, particularly among the fighting democats and demadogs.

Dear Director General,
 I write to draw your attention to the scandalous blackout which managed to switch me off from the entire population not only of England but of Europe, Australia and the United States in the crucial sleep-walking scene when I played Lady Macbeth in the production you broadcast last week. You must know just how much work went into this play, from the direction to the players and the technicians. Personally I did not, as you must appreciate, accept the role for the fee, which was nominal, but to reach this wider audience, in other words, for the greater glory of the art.
 In the name of both Shakespeare and all my fellow-workers I must protest vehemently at this totally unacceptable technical breakdown. I insist moreover that the play be rebroadcast, with all the non-star participants paid as for a repeat, as soon as you have managed to repair your transmitters.
                    Yours sincerely,
                         Paula James, D.B.C.

We are all flooded with thousands of such diskettes in both radio and television, mostly from furious listeners and viewers, but also from performers and wordprocessors. Dame Paula's letter is typical enough. Dear old Paula, she even wrote it herself in handwriting! Tim said to me after a meeting where it was read out as a sample: Just like the old days in Cornwall, never quite with it.

All letters naturally assumed that the sudden cuts were entirely our fault, our most grievous technical fault. So did the press, gloating at our discomfiture. A general wail of self-righteous reproach went up. Then, in fact fairly soon, when it became clear that something else was at stake since it was happening more and more often and to all radio and television stations in Europe, in America, all over the world, the wail of self-righteous reproach swelled slowly, though surprisingly slowly, to a generalised howl of rage. Unsurprisingly, but even more slowly than all the others, because always so confidently unaware, the politicians are the angriest. For their howl of rage, while claiming to be most concerned with the distressing and even dangerous gaps in both our cultural heritage and the diffusion of vital information, betrays by its tone that what is being experienced most deeply as intolerable in an age corresponding for decadence to the late Middle Ages, is the fact of such frequent and sudden losses in the eternal commentary.

As a one-time classicist, I don't have to wonder what people did in ancient times. They met in small numbers. They discussed. They read. They wrote. Commentary would grow and grow as each civilisation declined. But before the electromagnetic waves that we discovered we could generate as support for words of every kind, at every level, in all languages, always the same words, the same images violent and venal and revered, thrown far further afield than they ever could have been in an amphitheatre or an agora, before all this, what did people do? They talked. And the greatest displacements of world consciousness were achieved not in public, on worldwide screens, but in solitude, against the familiar forms of the eternal commentary, filched and reaffixed, refurbished and floundered around.

And now, for more than a century, the eternal commentary weighs heavy upon the air, overloading the waves with tetravocal news bulletins like modern operas, fast rolling Spanish over crisp Serbocrat under pompous English inexorably heard behind the French or vice-quadriversa. Inexorable? Tim once said at a meeting, nonsense, exore it at once. Though he told me privately that radio-astronomers have long been protesting at the drastic reduction of their universe-scrutinising possibilities down to an ever-narrowing beam. But surely mere quantity, even if it can physically dip and twist the frequencies agonisingly out of shape – but that's a mere metaphor, Tim says – couldn't explain these sudden stops. Fused noises, yes, and atmospherics, but not silence, except from trouble at the transmitter, and not all transmitters in the world could so frequently and simultaneously be in trouble. And why aren't words being garbled as on a tape at the wrong speed, or scrambled? But no, just silence.

It is as if the world had suddenly come to the conclusion that from now on it must eat its words. As if man must eat his words, all of them.

In fact the press soon named the whole phenomenon Verbivore. Some journalists tried Logophagoi – which pleased me more, as an ex Greek scholar, and also recalled the Xorandor affair with its Alphaphagoi, soon corrupted to Alphaguys – but it was too learned, or else rapidly reduced to Logfag by the more and more numerous who have no sense of etymology and therefore can't spell. But that's another problem, a lost cause. Be that as it may – and screentyping makes one verbose – Verbivore was easier to grasp, and therefore became more popular.

But who or what is doing the eating? Technically, we all learnt at the many meetings we have to attend, the very concept is impossible. You can intercept, but this naturally does not affect reception. And you can jam. But you cannot, at least not on this scale, suppress altogether, unless a generalised, worldwide network of transmitter-sabotage is assumed, and that, though a possibility, has unimaginably far-reaching technical, administrative and political implications. Meanwhile, we are all to continue as if our productions and presentations were being broadcast whole as before, in other words, as if nothing were happening. As I used to say, we'll all go on as if.

However, being at least partially responsible for the Xorandor episode, I can't help remembering, and thinking about it. And I feel sure that Tim is, if I dare use the phrase, on the same wave-length, since he was so involved in Xorandor. Press memory is remarkably short, because journalists are always so young, and so trained to be dramatic, that they tend to think everything is unprecedented. Even financial correspondents talk about an alltime low for the dollar, because they themselves have not experienced it lower (or higher), or can't remember a lower low even five years earlier. Tim and I are both older, and we are closely concerned, he as Managing Director, me as Drama Producer. The difficulty is, to meet him. He's so overwhelmed with the problem that he lives, as it were, in another world from mine.

Talking of protesting wordprocessors, it's Perry Hupsos, the author of that last radio-play I produced, who puzzled me the most. He seemed to have written the cut into his script. When I first read it, before Verbivore had seriously begun, I assumed the hero just dies suddenly, and although I didn't think much of that as an ending, I preferred not to question it, Perry being one of those touchy authors. But now it looks very different. Almost as if he had a premonition. Shades of Cassandra! But many wordprocessors have said they've imagined whole scenes that subsequently happened to them. Interestingly enough, though, as author, he took care not to cut his own play till very near the end, I mean it was commissioned as a thirty-minute play and couldn't have gone on more than five minutes at most. The joke was on him in the end, since the broadcast version was cut earlier, by Verbivore, whatever that is.

Odd bod. He went through a phase of calling himself Perry Striker, for some of his more social fictions anyway, as an (ironic?) gesture towards that old Soviet masquerade, a somewhat stained glaznost, many years ago. Shows how little Greek he knows, let alone Russian, but it caught on like wild old myths, and served him well. Then the phase passed as the word did, with the phenomenon, as in all things.

At any rate, after the broadcast Perry rang me up, furious. It's amazing how wordprocessors can get lost in their processing and have no idea what's happening in the world around them. They don't even seem to read the papers. He hadn't heard of Verbivore at all, although everyone was talking about it. A wordprocessor commissioned to process a radio-play who doesn't even bother to listen to the radio, or to other radio-plays. And this one about noise, too. It's true he had a good notion of how the sound-effects function and what the stereoworkshop can do, but then he's done radio-plays before.

I wonder what happened to Jip and Zab. Tim might know. I wish I could see him. But he's inordinately busy, all the more because he's such an expert on waveguides and microwaves and all the rest of it. Life, marriage, death and all the rest of it, as a literary Nobel Prize winner said in a radio-interview the other day, just before being, even him, cut. All the cuts are now being studied to see if there are patterns of occurrence. The above collection is culled from these recordings, which are typed out (and sometimes misunderstood and misspelt), then computeranalysed and handed out to us with incomprehensible graphs and statistics, in case anyone of us notices anything the technicians wouldn't know. Unlikely. And, of course, like everyone else, I have taken to typing things down, communicating with my personal computer through lack of the comforting pseudo-presences in the sitting-room, with their eyes on the telecue not you. Wordprocessing has become a withdrawal symptom.

If the eternal commentary disappears altogether in this way, if it is swallowed, or has to be given up through interference, won't mankind go slowly mad? Or shall we simply turn back to reading and writing and talking and behaving as if the media had never been? But that's no longer an option, I believe, our minds and psyches, our entire nervous system and networks of expectations have been transformed by the media. It is as if the electric waves of our brains had been altered by the electromagnetic waves around us, as if some anode had converted them into sound sense. We depend on the media for our lifeblood, the stream of information, the adventures, the violence, the romance, the games, the idols, the beauty, the knowledge, the gossip, all that Plato called Love Truth and Beauty, the explanations, the wooing of our beliefs, the eternal commentary that lines our lives like a loving companion, a double, making sense of it for us in its fragmentary and fragmented fashion.

Different people are angry about different bits of this lifeblood, this plasma, not about the bits as such but about their bad quality, their incompleteness. The young are hardly concerned since music, Fling, Broody, Jazz or Classical, is mysteriously unaffected, only words. Perhaps we shall have to sing our news bulletins and interviews. But no, presumably words when sung are left uncut because unrecognisable as words by whoever or whatever is word-eating. Anyway, only spoken words are affected. And the young don't view or listen to word-programs of any kind. So they can enjoy their hyperdaelic videoclips in peace, if peace is the term. And most of them don't miss the crap that's jockey-jabbered between discs. So the young don't care, as usual with major crises. The sofa-sportsmen are furious, and housewives are beside themselves without their ever increasing daily ration of soap. The old and the lonely are the most unhappy, they miss the comedy-programs, the plays, the phone-ins, the serials and games, the chat-shows, the documentaries, the old films. Everything in fact, that substitutes for company. But nobody takes much notice of the old and lonely, they rarely vote.

I miss none of that, but I am personally affected since I've always been a radio-addict, leaving the talk-stations on all night, and talking soothes me. I'm like Decibel, who seems to thrive on hifalutin discussions in a civilised tone. Buzz buzz buzz, oo, do go on. At first they take my mind physically out of its inner circles by making it follow whatever's being talked about. Then it slides off the phrases to the drone of that best narcotic, vox humana. But now alas, even the B.B.C. has extended its music-programs and is doing more and more just-disc sessions, like the rest of the stations at night, or even, since the crisis, by day.

The most peeved, as I said, are the politicians who, astonishingly, must have really relished the media and believed their own empty, confused and therefore often ungrammatical sentences. And to their chagrin their prestations are the least missed, except by each other and the journalists who are convinced that their obsessions about in-moves are shared by the rest of the population. And now, thank Verbivore, they are, at least on and off. No politician likes to have his words eaten by someone else, he's more used to having to do it himself.

The media! I say the media, meaning like everyone else radio as listened to publicly and television as viewed, because I'm part of them. But will other extensions of ourselves be touched? Will everything electromagnetic or microwavish be perturbed? Planes use radio and radar, so do spacestations and warships and teleguided trains and cars and – the vista is endless. Shall we all be cut off from each other, except in presence?

And today I have been in the presence, in the presence of Sir Timothy Lewis, Deputy-Director-General. I don't know why I felt he must have moved so far out of my world, I only had to ask for the interview to occur.

Yes, he said, I thought of it too. But only fleetingly, I must admit, as an outside, a very much outside possibility. The creatures were sent off the planet after all. And there are so many others.

Others?

Other possibilities.

What are they? Or perhaps you can't tell me.

Of course I can, but they're highly technical and –

I wouldn't understand.

You would, Mira my dear, but it would take time and – no don't complete my sentence, it would sound like a reproach again, unless I say it myself. As you must know, I'm under tremendous pressure, from all sides, up, down and sideways. All the responsible staff will be told at each stage when this or that hypothesis begins to look a little more than surmise, but there's no point in loading you all with the details of all our research in multiple directions. Everyone's been given the occurrence-charts and probability calculations – and of course any non-technical ideas, such as this one of yours, or political or whatever, from anyone, are welcome.

Yes, thank you. But we can't make much of charts without technical abilities, and hundreds of non-technical ideas have been put around already, here and in the press, some of them supercranky. Surely you have narrowed it down to a few hypos?

The main two are of course world-pollution and enemy action.

Your tone puts the same sort of scare-quotes round the word enemy that one still hears and sees around the words reality, soul, unconscious, democracy and other hypothetical entities in popular books on literature and philosophy. Are you still in touch with Jip and Zab?

No. Kids are rarely loyal to childhood adorations later in life, they're kind of ashamed I suppose. Jip read physics at Cambridge, so presumably he went in for it, and got high in the discipline, so he could be found in Who's Who. Wait a minute, I think I read somewhere, years ago, that he'd gone to Nasa. Another braindrain. But it can be checked.

And Zab?

No idea. She wanted to do philosophy.

She can't have succeeded then, philosophy and all the humanities disappeared from University programs in favour of hitec and science round about that time.

True. Poor old auntie B.B.C. inherited that torch and we're almost the only – I don't know why I said 'poor', Mira, forgive me.

You don't have to interpret my looks. And we're not the only ones, it's just that these subjects have merely become hobbies. Even Modern Languages teach only Technical Translation and Jargon. But you'll find these hobbies still in popular books and magazines. If you ever read such things.

Touché. But Zab was as scientifically gifted as her brother, even, I thought, more brilliant, more intuitive, though erratic. She would have done well in any branch. But I'm sure we can trace them both.

You don't have much time, Tim, would you like me to do the donkey-work? That's really why I came to see you, to find out if there might be anything in it, that would make tracing them worth while.

Of course my dear. No stone unturned, as it were.

Biggleton said that! Jesuscrumbs!

What?

No, sorry, that's from a louche character in a radio-play. But how idiotic of me. Dame Paula! She's their mother. She'd know.

Mira, but how idiotic of ME! I knew her well, I should have remembered. I'll write to her. Or no, I'll give her a ring, if you can find me her –

Don't you think, after that letter of hers and your possibly bland or technical reply, if any, that I should do it, for ostensibly personal reasons? I mean, your position might give the whole thing more credence than –

You're right. I leave it to you then.

3

Which was just as well, since I don't really have to go very far to find Zab, who remembers exactly what she was doing when she first heard of Verbivore. I can simply call her up, Isabel Manning, Euro-M.P. for Aachen International District, on account of her dual nationality, fluent French and German, and a higher technological competence than most M.P.'s. After all, she had taught Communications for years at the Technische Hochschule in Aachen. She's lucky, most Euromps have to live in their constituencies and keep travelling to the new European Parliament in Aachen, a town better known outside Germany, or at least in France, as Aix-la-Chapelle, one-time centre of an early undivided Europe of sorts. And that name was officially chosen to pacify France, Belgium and Luxemburg, all furious when the Community, numbering twenty-three and tired of seeing its resources drained by the communications wastage of having three capitals, outvoted them for a radical reorganisation and one capital only, in Aix-la-Chapelle, the entire area around it being internationalised into a sort of European Washington DC. The French ironically call it Washington d'ici. But Zab's constituency is the new international district.

She remembers because she was trying to recall an incident from her childhood. And, in peculiar fact, the shadowy impossible possibility of Verbivore came to her unofficially via her son, age eighteen, long before the so-called beginning or "first day", as it was later retrospectively aetiologised.

The reason she was trying to remember this childhood incident was that although she had carefully entered it into the computer she and Jip had at the time, she had no memory of it whatever when she called it up, by chance, on that April day some twenty years later, twenty-three years to be exact, and this bugged her. She even wondered whether she had invented it, but it kind of rang true: at fourteen her interests had been far more scientific than fictional – if such an old-fashioned distinction can still be made.

Zab lives in a small flat just beyond the second ring around Aachen, behind a wooded hill called the Lousberg, not from Laus or louse, they say, but from some Louis or other. There are no houses on the Lousberg side of her street. Instead, steps go up a steep grass bank into the wood. It's like having a forest at my door, she says to her friends, and I can walk over the hill through the wood and down the other side into the inner town. For Aachen, although it has a large suburbia and a wide outer ring, and an even wider Autobahn surround, is itself small. I remember earlier on, she tells them, trying to buy a skirt-hook in what seemed the inner town and being told I'd only find such a small thing *in der Stadt*. But I am in the town, I said. They meant the old town, the innerest, within the innerest ring, an inner sanctum one can walk across in about ten minutes. But I suppose the real inner sanctum must be the remains of Charlemagne's chapel inside the cathedral, the quark to Aachen's atom.

And outwards from this atom, linked by the electromagnetic force of a complex Autobahnkreuz, are other atoms, some of which Aachen now almost touches, Düren and Köln to the East, Düsseldorf to the North-East, Bonn and Koblenz to the South-East, Liège or Lüttich or Luik to the West, Heerlen and Antwerp to the North-West. For Aachen, despite its new status and revived old French name, lies in what is still called *Dreiländereck*, on the old German frontier with both Holland and Belgium.

When I came to live here she types into her processor, my twin-brother John wrote to me as Alcuina, at the Court of Charlemagne, Aix-la-Chapelle – though he did also put in the street and number in order to reach me.

Why have I typed "my twin-brother John" instead of Jip,

as if I were writing this for other eyes? The private memoir, the diary or the journal habit, even private letters, decayed so completely as a form of communication during the public electronic age that we fall back, when we want to use it again, on antiquated formulas we then still studied at school, the secret journal really meant for publication and posterity. Yet who would ever have brought out a Compact Disc called the Collected Telephone Conversations of say, Christa Wolf or Woody Allen, as they used to bring out The Collected Letters, the Journal, The Diary of?

Yet clearly I am deriving pleasure, just as fiction-writers used to, from the mere noting of facts, instead of getting to the point. *Zur Sache! Zur Sache!* The real Sache being, however, the day I learnt about the Logophagoi and its resulting passionate return to writing. How to come *zur*? Ah yes, the attic.

There are few houses in my street, since it's short and ends in a field at the foot of the Lousberg, but they're all fairly comfortable, and we're surrounded with gardens and greenery. My view East from the living-room terrace at the back is downhill over more posh houses, more posh gardens, then the Football Stadium and the famous Reitstadion, then the Bubble, the huge and hideous Eurocomplex, though some find it beautiful, under which spread the high, the low, the round, the rectangular, the pyramidal buildings of the European Parliament, Economic Council, and the rest, as well as reception halls, luxury flats for the top people, comfortable sleeping quarters for late workers, shopping centres, gardens, tennis-courts, mini-golf, swimming, sauna, the lot, the entire set-up air-conditioned and protected from the summer heat and the cold North German winters. The diplobubble, die Hochbeamtenblase or Bürokratenblase, la bulle des baratineurs or bulleburotique, the hotair bubble, la bollatura in Italian with a nice pun, and so on. Of course no one actually lives there. Ambassadorial ranks have grand apartments in town (all the old humanities buildings were pulled down for these) or houses outside town, inasmuch as there is an outside now that doesn't merely become another town. But many Euromps like to find a pad in the Bubble for their visits, which then seem a bit like a luxury holidaycamp to them, especially when they're coming from wintry climates. The rest, the interpreters, secretaries, computer-clerks and so on, live in less upmarket high-rise buildings to the North and West of the town, invisible from here. The Bubble is also called the Blister, or la Cloque, or la Cloche à Fromage, by those who think it an eyesore. Beyond the diplobubble eastwards, low hills can be glimpsed through the glaznostic bubble between the buildings.

My flat is on the second floor of one of those old bourgeois houses built in the nineteen-eighties, but it's also the top flat, smaller than the other two flats below in that it's already in the roof, with dormer-windows and sloped ceilings, and a little terrace above part of my neighbours' much more spacious living-room. But from the small entrance hall a narrow flight of stairs leads up to a splendid chalet-like attic as large as the house, with a huge roof-window. It used to be Hanjo's room. It has now become my teleport.

Is all this detail necessary? Offline tapeworm, as Jip used to call me when I did this during our creation of Xorandor, as if it were important to say we had Cornflakes for breakfast. Why does it seem vital to get my topographical position so exactly right, simply because I live here, simply because it's real to me? It means damn all to anyone else and probably doesn't even evoke a vague image. What have we lost, or what are we all trying to hold onto or recapture since the disappearance of books? Everything being on hard disc or diskette now, with content invisible so that only maniac readers buy them. And now, the Logophagoi (the Logfaggots as some illiterates are already deforming).

I was up there, on a cool Sunday in April, at last trying to sort out all my old Quatsch and make discroom for new Quatsch. I started with the oldest stackfile of floppies, as they used to be called. Most of the labels were clearly marked as to content and I could judge by the callcodes alone whether to efface them or not, or even to throw them away altogether – for naturally I had no time to screen them all just to decide. The really old ones – why can't I dump anything? – belonged to older computers anyway, possibly too old even for the interface on my Intercompatible. Handshake, the interfacing used to be called, as if computers had hands to shake or faces to inter. But the real reason was time. Rummaging in an attic always has its temptations and I was determined to be ruthless. Then I found a diskette, and its clumsy size at once took me right back to our childhood – Jip's and mine. But the callcodes on the label were incomprehensible. They'll be incomprehensible even in a few years, Jip used to say of my secretive ways, you'll have forgotten. I won't, I won't! But I have. A few years? Nearly a quarter of a century! LOOP, ZBX, LM, SCAN, FLOAT, OLDF, NEWF, GO. Well, they're mostly computerms, but I must have used them as codes for something else so knowing that doesn't help. What content did they convey, what text would they call up on the screen? As for the initials, ZBX, LM, GQ...? GQ? Ghastly Quarters? Geopolitical Quiz? The Gist of Quarks? Gigo Quatsch? Gormless Quibble? German Quarrel? That faint-connected. I realised the diskette must date back to our year-and-a-half stay in Bayreuth after the hooha (swags! thunks! and all that diodic bootstrap we random-jittered!). I guess some of it stuck. Would I understand it? Would my Intercompatible read it? It has an entry for old large discs at the back somewhere.

Nothing for it, I had to try. Clearly I couldn't keep all these floppies. But this one I knew I must see first. So in it went. Großer Quertreiber? Grausame Quälen? Grenzlose Quackelei? The Handshake worked in a few nanoseconds. File. Öffnen.

> Spaghetti logic array with Herr Groenitz tonight. He was drunk. Frieda said so later, daran muss Du nicht mehr denken, er war schwer betrunken. Is that an excuse? (Sorry says some button-pushing prez, I was drunk). Booleshit, stop being such a Tugendheldin. Prig, much shorter. Using English cos no scharfes s on Poccom keyboard. Okay Erzählung.
>
> Meal went fine as usual with Rudi and Jip and me making maybe too much noise. Rudi's Vater – why do we call his mother Frieda but his father sein Vater oder Herr Groenetz? Well, Frieda's more friendly and in fact mum's friend, whereas Herr Groenetz had never met mum and dad till they came last summer and he seemed

to take an instant dislike to dad. Jealousy perhaps, he's only a Diplomierter Ingenieur (in fact we privately call him Dipling because he has Dipl. Ing. on his van), whereas dad's a physicist and got lots of attention through the Xorandor hooha. But he's much older than Frieda, a whole generation older at least, and there seem to be a few dangling refs to WW II somewhere in his datanetwork, or maybe learnt from his father, who would have been old enough to have been fascistically active then. At any rate mum had told us to avoid politics, as he's now a bit too rabidly at the other end of the spectrum and a bit too self-righteously spouting commycat with tramline symptoms.

Commycat? What the megavolt was that? I found myself using our old slang. Tramline symptoms, that was Jip's term for ideological crap blindly repeated by the brainwashed, and it tends to be at the extremes that people need to be told what to think, so when they have to give up one extreme for some reason they veer to the other. So commy must be communist. Yes: He's an old commy, I'd once said to mum on a visit and she'd vaguely echoed oh yes, very crummy. Commycat. Like copycat? Then I remembered: communist catechism. But who was I, then, to call it so self-righteously "self-righteously"? Next screen.

At any rate, we studiously avoided politics as usual, and as usual stuck to smalltalk Quatsch when not making Spassquatsch with Rudi. But we'll never learn proper German if we stick to the weather and schooltalk. So when Dipling started talking about dad showing fascist strains and being moreover in danger of becoming a Fachidiot, Jip jumped in, tho Frieda kept trying to tone it all down and change the subject and telling her husband to stop downing one Bierkrug after another, which were later followed by whiskies in quick succession.

The thunkish thing was that he seemed to loadlink so easily on dad as a way of NOT talking politics, but of course to him the whole boolesup Welt is politics, and he grabbed at dad, on and on, less and less loyally or even politely, gleefully nasty, and all punctuated by expressions of how he was only saying this out of concern, for dad, for mum, for us, and how "wir" had all carefully avoided the topic (dad) yet "couldn't help" bringing it up (es ging gar nicht anders). Whereas we'd pounced on it (Jip defending dad but also partly agreeing) in order on the contrary to avoid politics!

This until Frieda insisted we change the subject. But all was reasonably floatpoint and jokestacked till then, nor did I comment on how offline and unspooling his terminal display was.

As I read, I remembered suddenly how in the middle of the hooha someone, Alex I think, had said we'd become spoilt brats if we were allowed to go to the nuclear station, especially if we succeeded in saving the situation (and of course if we didn't we'd be dead like everyone around). Did we become spoilt brats? I sure struck myself now, reading this, as a precocious prig.

We were sitting around after the meal in the living-room, when Dipling asked if the Greens were popular in England, or rather, why they weren't a bigger movement, deforestation and all that. No, Jip and Rudi had gone up to Rudi's room to play computergames (Rudi the older is still at the game-stage), so I was alone with Dipling and Frieda, anxious to get more conversation practice. Man vs. Frau and mere schoolgirl. But I thought this topic as stated safe enough, so I leapt in, saying how they don't have as much Erfolg as in Germany and haven't pierced through into Parliament, tho of course all parties paid Greenlipservice. And I launched into an explanation of the English electoral system which doesn't allow small parties to get in – all this more as German practice than to impart info, which I suppose he knew – when suddenly he started.

DIP: The nadir was reached by Wilson and Callaghan.
ME: (*Surprised, still with deforestation and electoral system, and not at all sure who Wilson and Callaghan were – they sounded like a music-hall turn*) What nadir?
DIP: Well, the moral nadir.
ME: But what do you mean by the moral nadir?
DIP: Well, the moral degradation.
ME: (*Still friendly but teasing*) Hey, dad'd say here you're like the young, who can't define their generalisations except with other generalisations. WHAT moral degradation? (*Course he isn't young, so dad's wrong on that, must be more the semi-literate of any age and time. But that seemed to flatter him, or at least to flipflop the possible danger of mentioning dad, into mere repeat*)
DIP: Well, the appalling policies.
ME: (*Laughing now*) How long does this go on? WHAT appalling

policies? (*Also hoping it will come out without my having to show my ignorance of who Wilson and Callaghan were, and what they had to do with deforestation*).
FR: Go on Liebchen, be specific! (Drück Dich genauer aus!)
DIP: Well, all the bullshit (Quatsch).
ME: WHAT bullshit?
DIP: (*Angry, downing more whisky*) THE bullshit, all the bullshit.
ME: (*Still amused by this stepwise unrefinement but thinking it just a game or drunken bootstrap*) Come on, Herr Groenetz, tell us what you have in mind.
DIP: You tell ME what YOU have in mind.
ME: (*Bootloaded by aggressive tone*) I have nothing in mind, I'm asking YOU to define what YOU mean by the terms YOU've been using, from nadir to bullshit.
DIP: (*Calmer*) Well, their sell-out to America.
ME: (*Total bootstrap about England's American policies at whatever period he's buffering on about and genuinely wanting to know, so unaware of scare-signs*) But in what way were their policies towards America appalling? (*I used his terms*) What sell-out?
DIP: (*To Frieda*) WE understand each other. It's clear she doesn't.
FR: But Liebchen, she's scarcely fourteen!
ME: No I don't understand. (*Making attempt to clear things up*) You brought up the subject, whatever it is, and you've steadily refused to tell me what it is, so I tried teasing it out of you. There's no reason to get angry.
DIP: I can't accept this kind of specious argument.
ME: Specious argument! It's you who's being specious. I haven't used ANY argument, I've asked you what you meant by nadir and bullshit and after a Viertelstunde I finally get sell-out to America. But we were talking about the Greens and deforestation and the electoral system. So I was simply flummoxed, and still am. Or non-plussed, as Xorandor would say.
DIP: (*very angry*) There you go again, with your vanity and your specious arguments.
FR: Calm down... We probably all agree anyway, we're all against the missiles.
ME: (*Bootstrapped with astonishment! Realising too late that we're on his tramlines again and that I must do everything to change the subject or clear out but how?*)
DIP: No, I object!
FR: Object to what? She hasn't said anything.
DIP: I object to the word p-p-probably (W-w-wahrscheinlich).

ME: There's nothing wahrscheinlich about it. On the contrary, she's quite sure to say "But the Russians are worse".
ME: (*Here all my sofar funface attitude froze into fury and I became hexadex miffed rather than quizzy. I looked all round the room, under the sofa, got up to open the sideboard with pointed irony*) Russians? Where? Who mentioned Russians? Is there someone else here?
DIP: (*Furious*) Du freches Kind! How dare you talk to me like that? You think you know everything because you got into the papers last year over that ridiculous adventure of yours. Lady Macbeth he's supposed to have called himself, all a put-up job if you ask me. You know perfectly well what I mean.
ME: I know NOW, though it took me twenty minutes to get it out of you. (*Angry now too*) By what right d'you claim to know what I'm GOING to say, what's in MY mind, when I haven't said anything to give you any kind of clue, and only asked you what you meant? By what right d'you plonk me into a ready-made category when you weren't even capable of telling me clearly and straight out what was in YOUR mind? I may be a child but I won't have this kind of stupid labelling.
DIP: (*Suddenly lost*) Your sort, offspring of elites, always using specious arguments.
ME: I did NOT, repeat NOT, use ANY arguments. I was asking questions. We're not elitist offspring, that's loopy (blöd) but in my family we argue in a civilised tone and define our terms (*Not sure this wholly true, but it's true enough compared with him, and sounded good*).
DIP: (*Roused again and really shouting now*) Your family! It's because of people like you and your brother and your father that we're going straight into another world war.
ME: (*Suddenly very calm*) If you really believe that, then you have no business receiving us in your house. (*Exit me, to hall, followed by wailing Frieda who says he doesн't mean it etc but I shake her off and walk out of the house slamming the front door*).

Well of course I had to come back, after walking around Bayreuth for a couple of hours to faint strains of openair Götterdämmerung or something from the Wagner festival which had just started, and hoping they'd be gigavolt anxious. But it's late July and the days are still long. I did ragingly think of a few bold hitchhiking and stowaway schemes back to Cornwall, but storming out in a huff isn't really me. So instead, I've been sitting up recording it while it's all wortwörtlich in my mind.

END GQ

4

I still didn't know what GQ stood for (Groenetz Quarrel?) but at least I now knew its content, and its incredible silliness. I wondered briefly how soon after this I had learnt not to pounce on insults, and the general uselessness of saying things straight out as I felt and thought them, or even of insisting on the opponent's weak logic. I also remembered what computer whizz-kids Jip and I had been (now they're a dime a dozen) and how edge-triggering this must have been to many people such as Groenetz or even Rudi. But all this I shrugged off, for what scared me more than anything was that I couldn't remember this scene at all. I couldn't remember storming out. I couldn't remember coming back to what must have been Frieda's relieved and tearful reproaches. I couldn't remember typing the quarrel into the computer. And it was my own hidden, secret floppy, I remembered that, and its mystery callcodes. Clearly I didn't tell Jip about the quarrel the next day, nor, presumably, did anyone else mention it, or I'd have recalled it from pseudo-memory afterwards.

Naturally lots of gigo went in, for fun, for practice, and I felt sure that if I called up the other texts I'd have repeat experiences. Perhaps they might recall other things that would bring back the experienced reality of this scene. But I couldn't understand how such an incident could have been completely deleted from my mind, erased ROM as I used to say. It seemed to me I should have remembered at least the fact of the quarrel if not the content. Or a difficult atmosphere with Herr Groenetz. But no, all was sweetness and light in my memory of our long stay in their house. Plato said the technique of writing would cause men to lose their memories in favour of memorability, what would he say about computers? We externalise not only our memories into them but our already weak capacities for logic. Still, it's just as well we don't clutter our memories with the stupidities. The twentieth century went loopy with the idea that all the bad things must be recaptured and thereby exorcised. Which was, in a more concrete sense, exactly what I had just done with the floppy, poor unconscious dump. But I didn't feel a bit exorcised.

In any case the Xorandor affair, then as yet unfinished, must have completely engrossed us, even though we'd been sent out there to forget it and to be out of the way of the journalists till it had all died down. Also of course, going to school in Bayreuth and learning not just German but everything else in German must have absorbed all our energies. Rather like the mixed bag of students I used to have at the Technische Hochschule, some of them very bright, others hopeless, who came and still come from all over the world to learn microelectronics or physics or political economy but who have to learn it in German. Seems so unfair, why the double effort, why don't we go out to them and learn their languages? Well, we do, but we're no good at them so it's less efficient. Of course they've all produced their own teachers and technical schools, but there's still this myth of Western technical (if no other) superiority that dies hard, though the Senegalese, for instance, and the West Indians, are vastly superior, not to mention the Koreans, the Japanese, the Chinese and more or less all the South-East Asians.

Silent typing sure encourages loquacity, I'll have to scrap all that if I want to keep this record. What I did know, and could never forget, was that the whole story of Xorandor had gone into Poccom 3, both then, in Bayreuth, and after we got back to Cornwall, and although I made Jip promise to delete the whole thing after Xorandor told us his secret – or his possible lie (who knows?) – I later learned that he hadn't. I wondered then whether he ever intended to use the info. He always said not, or rather, we never talked about it but he acted as if it had gone as agreed. So why had he kept it? But he became very devious, like most nuclear physicists.

I remember thinking this aloud, and hearing myself say that last remark with a slight shock.

How long ago it all seemed to me then, as I sat in my teleport staring at the last screen of text down to END GQ, pointlessly trying to remember that pointless German Quarrel. And how longer ago its causes seemed, the American missiles in Europe! And as for Wilson and Callaghan, softshoe duo or comic turn, they'd been I think Prime Ministers ages before I was even born. I evidently never bothered to learn exactly what they'd done about the missiles, but presumably they let them in. And then the long, long Doppelnull and other negotiations that began with or soon after the Xorandor affair. The Eastern block, as it was then called, is now no longer really a block but a loose federation of free-trading nations, free trade and local elections being perhaps the only freedom it was at last allowed. Because it did, slowly, surreptitiously, for its own economic survival, introduce reforms towards commercial and industrial competition that made the differences between it and the West look like a mere matter of slightly changed political labels. (They even had to let westerly satellites join Europe, as well as Finland and Austria which had some sort of special status that had prevented them, but not of course Bulgaria or Romania). They call it Post-Socialism, which somehow manages to imply that Socialism is both dead and very much alive. Like Post-Feminism, Post-Democracy, Post-Humanism, Post-Commitment and the rest.

And yet the type of dummes Argument, as apparently produced then only by an elderly drunk, now seems almost the norm, and the fixation of positions I know hasn't changed at all, but rather got steadily cruder and wider, and also upward-spread, gaining in respectability what it never had in sweet reason or sharp logic. Forty years of deterrent had kept the peace, at least between the so-called big powers, but now almost thirty years of dedeterrent (and the twentieth century began all those de-words that implied the wrongness of previously approved policies, from denazification and decolonisation to denationalisation, deprivatisation, decentralisation, deregulation etc) have also kept that same peace, so neither theory is proven, and each is dangerous. The big powers have more or less disarmed, at least to the diplomatic satisfaction of mutual but fairly well organised verification teams. Glaznostalgia, people call it now. However, every smaller terrorist state has its own superwarheads, happily sold to them by the big powers' armament industries. The problem of the deterrent has merely been displaced to the irresponsible and the fanatical. What is Xorandor thinking now, I wondered, or has he died out on Mars, from insufficiency of natural radiation? For of course the politicians did not keep their promise of providing him and his offspring with nuclear waste to feed on, it was too expensive as a solution. Did he tell the truth about his origins and are there as he said innumerable Xorandors of all ages and aeons silently feeding on nuclear waste as well as on warheads and listening to us still all over the planet Earth?

I must have been in the middle of such musings when the doorbell rang. I left the attic and went down to the hall. Wer ist es? I asked the intercom. Mutti? – Hanjo! What – ? Come on up.

He'd got even taller, and looked more Chinese than ever. When I thought of him simply as an entity, an existence in my life, it was as my semi-oriental boy of seven or ten or twelve. When I saw him as a concrete presence now, at eighteen, I saw him more correctly, but what is correctly? The way someone is, at the moment, all at once, in front of you, is that more correct than all the other images? These odd impressions were presumably due to the fact that I was no longer bringing him up, accepting his allatonce-ness at every moment without shock of recognition. I busied myself with the tea, determined not to ask what he was doing in Aachen, or indeed in Europe, well before the end of even the American summer term, or why he hadn't let me know. Over tea he said,

I went down to see Uncle Jip in Texas.

Oh? How is he? Was it nice?

Very hot. Fine. Invited me down. Said he had an urgent packet for you he wanted delivered in person. Told me to skip the last three weeks of school, said he'd make up the data so's I could write my papers ahead of time, and jeenukes, he did, and I did. And here it is.

He'd been opening his back-pack and now he handed me a small squarish padded envelope.

How mysterious. But don't you have to do exams as well?

No, we get graded on practical and theoretical stuff all year round. Lots of students have to earn money for school in the summer months so –

I was gazing at Jip's padded envelope as he talked. A diskette, clearly. Addressed in mock-mediaeval script to Alcuina, Aix-la-Chapelle, by hand of Hanjo. Who was talking about his college, his trip to Texas, and what he was going to do this summer. I listened, proud, amazed, dismayed, proud. I'm hitchhiking a long flight to China, he said, through a pilot friend. Aren't you going to open it?

Later.

Uncle Jip said it was urgent.

If it's waited till you got here it can wait a few hours more. Why China? But I knew.

To find my father.

It's a big country. Over a million million.

Not all males, not all the same age, not all from Shensi, not all called Chang-ti-lu, not all hitec. That cuts it down to about one hundred million or less. With the computers they have –

He only CAME from Shensi, which is as large as England, and very mountainous. He studied somewhere in Manchuria, Kirim Polytechnic I think, then Aachen. He could have been sent anywhere since then, from Kwangtung in the tropical South to Heilungkiang in the freezing North. And what will you do when you've found him?

Nothing. Just, get to know him. Why, why didn't you try to find him when you went on that data-determining trip in March?

Why should I? Oh I know, you've always suspected you were the chance result of a one-night stand, because he left. But it wasn't like that at all. We were both students here. I was eighteen. We had a brief, but passionate affair. It was over in peace and mutual esteem before he left, these things happen you know, and we never said goodbye, I never hated or cursed him or had terrible regrets or rebounds or anything like that, and today I'm thankful I didn't marry him, my life would have been totally different, and I like my life as it is.

But you never tried to contact him and tell him of my existence. You could have traced him through the University, or now through your diplo contacts.

They can't keep track of all their ex-students you know. I wasn't even sure that he was going back to China. He may be in America for all I know. My dear boy, you do have surprisingly old-fashioned notions compared to my generation. The conservative backlash I suppose, some of it welcome no doubt.

Society would collapse completely without the idea of the family, it's universal.

Yes darling. But it is simply an idea, a cultural development. Biologically there are only three factors, the two sexes, the sequence in births, and the succession of generations. Out of these mankind invented the family, necessary, as you so rightly say, to society. But there are many, many variations you know, even, somewhere or other, marriage between a fertile woman and a sterile woman, who takes over the man's role. But in my youth the bachelor mother was almost the norm, many women chose it as the ideal solution to the problems of marriage versus career. We took it in our stride. I went on with my studies. A child and a career, and occasionally a man, rather than a man, a child, and maybe a career. It has its points, and its losses.

For some reason this speech, reasonable though it sounds, if a little pompous, as here written (but by me of course, and six weeks later), led us straight into one of our cruel and bitter quarrels. Motherhood in your stride, that's just it, you strode through it, you were always striding out and away to some course or conference or fact-finding mission, as if facts had to be found. – Are you reproaching me for lack of love and attention? – No of course not, Mutti that's wimpy. – So what then? – You don't understand, you've never understood, you just go through the motions, you've wrapped yourself in a shell and I can't get through to you. – What shell? Be specific. – I can't. – You're talking nonsense darling. – As usual you're no doubt thinking. – Hanjo that's unworthy of you, how can you be so sure what I'm thinking when you've just complained you can't get through to me, be logical. – Be logical, always logical, I'm not a fucking computer, and don't say computers don't fuck they use partition, grow up out of your great childhood adventure Mutti, Uncle Jip's not like that at all, he never refers to it and he has a nice wife and three kids and it's a nice normal family. – So that's it, jealousy? – NO! – Don't shout, besides, that too isn't as diodic as it may look on the surface. – Isn't as WHAT? Is that your twin private language again, why do you still need to exclude, he doesn't. And so on. I ended up in tears, saying I'm sorry, I'm sorry, he first embarrassed then embracing, but not saying sorry. He wins, always, and I let him, though nothing is resolved for him. Peace then ensues, until the next time round.

The rest of the evening we discussed the practical aspects of his plan to go to China and find his father. Does he know German? Or English? Probably both, he certainly got to speak fluent German here, it was part of his assignment, not part of mine to learn Chinese alas, though he did teach me some ideograms. Good, then he shouldn't be hard to talk to. Right, but my love, promise me that if you do find him, you'll tell him this is entirely your idea, not mine. He promised. But then, so had Jip promised, in another context, once long ago.

Maybe I'm remembering it wrong, writing it down wrong. Maybe that speech on the family, which was intended and remembered as objective facts sweetly and gently presented, was received as Oh come off it, family's only an idea, you've always had a buzz in your brain about that, and tried to make me feel guilty whereas I, and so on. Maybe his accusations of striding out and away were really intended as But Mutti, there are also disadvantages to a fatherless family, I'm only trying to and so on. The tone of the human voice is such a give-away that not a word we utter can be received exactly as we're afterwards so convinced we meant to say it, nor, maybe, as we're so convinced beforehand and during that we are saying it. I suppose that only quarrels by letter or diskette can be analysed afterwards for just where and how the misunderstanding arose. But who keeps letters nowadays? And who doesn't efface diskettes? (Me!) And there too, in writing, and even in typing, there's also a tone, a rhetoric that betrays more than it says – otherwise there would have been no interpretation industry through the ages, abolished today as a waste of energy, time and teaching hours on mere multiplicity of readings.

And did rushing to one's computer at thirteen and a half after a quarrel to get it all down "wortwörtlich" make much difference? Perhaps there too I exaggerated. And that was a political, not a personal quarrel, and political quarrels on a larger scale lead to mass murder – in fact old Dipling accused me, and my family, of precisely that. Diplomatic quarrels, I thought, must be less naive, but still a question of facesaving. The side that's having its representatives expelled for "activities incompatible with" must know if the accusation is true or not, and expels the other side's representatives as pure reprisal. But reprisals can go very far, and nations sound like kids yelling who started. I remember one question Chang asked me, with exquisite courtesy all those nineteen or so years ago, about one such incident. But how can you be so sure that your country is legally or even morally in the right? Maybe it has other reasons, just as the other country has, for its behaviour. You are condemning the men expelled, without trial, only your government's word, which you are assuming is honourable, whereas the foreign country by definition must be lying. I tried to answer, it's because all the standards I was brought up on – rather strict for their time – have been stood on their heads by younger nations or nations whose different ethos we never bothered to learn. But I suppose it goes back a long way beyond my own lifetime or even my father's. I read somewhere that airmen in the First World War thought it rather UNFAIR to fly over enemy positions and photograph them. As for radio interception some people thought it totally immoral, only letters and messages hidden in walking sticks being fair game. Can you imagine? After all the regular interception and decoding everyone did for the rest of the century? But now, I said, for the last fifty years even the most powerful nations have been helpless in the face of primitive blackmail with hostage-taking and terrorism. I forget what happened in the particular case – they were as regular as clockwork in those days. The usual compromise no doubt. Like bursting into tears and being embraced. Yet wars, with their so far always acceptable mass murders, arise from not having achieved these diplomatic compromises. The blind self-justification and official face-saving that cover the passion are of the same nature in the person, in the family, in the neighbourhood, in the tribe, in the realm, the difference is only in scale of effects. Didn't Confucius-he-say something of the sort? Yet no one ever appears to himself wholly wrong in any of these disputes, from tiffs to wholesale massacres, since right at any one time, in any one place, is merely the same God-of-Old who's always on one's own side. And I thought again of that Xorandor text Jip had promised to erase.

I had left it to him because I had a broken arm at the time and was too busy learning to write with my left hand. But I know he didn't do it. I know because two years later, when he was rushed off to hospital with acute peritonitis, I was looking for an instruction-book he'd borrowed, and rummaging in his stuff. I found two floppies, marked X, carefully hidden among physics papers in a box. I stared at them. Fleeting butterfly queries were transformed pico into sharp suspicion.

No, the other way round, a sudden sharp suspicion called up fleeting butterfly queries. I checked, and there it was, our original Xorandor story, chatterboxy and unrevised. He must have copied the originals before erasing them to show them to me, callcoded Xorandor and empty. I felt sick with shock. Not because he had wanted to keep them – why not, maybe my request was unreasonable. Not even because he'd broken his promise. But because he had lied to me, and in such an elaborate way. I'm sure the peculiar change in our almost telepathic relationship dates back to that day, though I never said anything. But deeply hurt, I went in for a swift silent revenge. I told myself that if he wanted it kept I would do the keeping, and in exactly the same way. I transferred the content of both floppies onto one more comprehensive smaller disc for my new computer, giving it one of my mystery callcodes. I still have it with me, here in this very attic. I erased his floppies called X and put them back where I had found them, between exactly the same pages in exactly the same place, which had become marked on the paper from the weight of the physics notes. He never mentioned it, so presumably he has them somewhere in his Nasa office and has never called them up. Or else he has, and kept silent, assuming I erased them out of anger but also out of conviction. So which is worse? Not keeping a promise and cheating about it, or sneaking and cheating back, in the same way, out of revenge?

It was an awe-fully moral day, that day I first learnt about Verbivore. I felt rather a pompous ass, too. That night, after making up the bed in the teleport for Hanjo, I opened Jip's padded envelope. In it was a square carton with a diskette inside it (had he somehow also kept a copy?). And a short covering letter in handwriting:

Dear Zab,
I'm sending you this diskette by special messenger. You'll see why when you screen it. Please erase it after memorising the main facts. I want your reaction, but not in writing. I'll be in Europe in late June and will come and see you. Destroy this note.

I hope you're well. Hanjo's grown into a pleasant young man, though none too bright for someone who wants to do physics. He got on well with Ivor (10), took no notice of little Paul (8) and fell a bit in love with Willa (13) as cousins do at that age. I don't think he's a future scientist or even tecman. A poet perhaps, tho he can't spell, or a sociologist or maybe a politician. They're all much the same from our more rigorous viewpoint, but poets do less harm. Jeanie sends her love. Me too. See you soon.

Jip

The next day, after taking Hanjo to the bank to give him money for his journey, and driving him to the new international airport where his plane and pilot friend awaited, I got back to the solitude of my attic. More screens, and screens. A Nasa Report, TOPMOST TOP SECRET. Codename: SPEAKLOSS.

5

Jip has kept the habit of recording all meetings including private convs. The way he held his wrist forward all the time, he was obviously wearing a microrecording watch. But he never did like the work of actually narrating something afterwards. Just the salient facts, that's all he was interested in. If he has written down all we said afterwards, or typed it into his computer, I suppose it would be in telegraphic form with minimum comment. Unless he's caught the general need to express personal garbage in writing and tries. Like for instance:

Saw Zab this afternoon to tap her reactions. Hot still tho cooler than Texas. Cd've sat on her terrace, in shade by then, but didn't want to be overheard, even in English. Our twin-telepath seems very altered, has been altering over the years, what with different studies, languages, countries, nationalities now, and lives. She doesn't even look like me any more, so thin and taut. It's true I've filled out a bit. And somehow she's become a bit devious. No, he wouldn't say all that.

I recorded the dialogue, tiny mike and tape in my watch, can't trust my reconstruct, as we used to call it during X, and she always was better at it than me. Few prelims, I asked her almost straight out for her reaction.

My first fear was for Hanjo (she said), those plane-collisions I mean – he'd just left. But then I read on and saw they'd stopped. And soon got a phone-call he'd arrived.

You read, in the report you mean?

Well, yes.

But Zab, those plane-crashes in series were the talk of the time.

My second reaction was disbelief. About Verbivore I mean. I've been so busy, I simply hadn't noticed, and no one told me.

You're incredible, Zab. Everyone's talking about it. Don't your fellow M.P.'s discuss it in Parliament? Or on Committees? Or during rich lunches?

Oh, Parliament! I'm on an Agricultural Technology Committee and worked non-stop on an endless report. Besides, I was on an EEC data-determining mission to China in March.

And I suppose the data you determined, on the Wall and in The Forbidden City, were useful?

Oh don't you start! Anyway, I wasn't here. Not when the thing started getting really noticeable and talked about.

But didn't Hanjo say anything?

No. We talked – of other things.

But what about radio and television? You visibly have both.

Oh, I've stopped watching German TV, it's too boring, nothing but men shaking hands before meetings – still rarely women incidentally – or bits of a speech. That's for the reports, and otherwise it's a man or woman reading, turning visible pages. Visualised radio in fact. Has been for years. Part of an anti-star policy, pure info, no emotive identification. Idea good but result unwatchable. Rest is serials and old films.

But what about other countries, the rest of Europe, the States, Africa, the rest of the world?

It's all become what the French call politique politicienne, the insistent journalist needling a spokesman to speak what he won't. I mean for the news. Otherwise it's infinite variations on prize-winning games. Besides, if you don't want to spend hours zapping you have to spend a day scrutinising a World-TV journal to select. I do sometimes, and mark things, but then I forget.

Anyone who's dealing both with politics and hitec should keep herself informed.

I do, from reports on my Fach, and from seeing the people and the areas concerned. TV's been going steadily downhill, every cliché question and reaction and public indignation expected as programmed.

You're an intellectual snob, no wonder you're out of touch.

55

It's not snobbery, it's observation. Stop bullying me, Jip.
Well, what's your reaction now?
I agree with you.
I haven't expressed an opinion yet.
No. But you sent me the secret Nasa sitrep, at great risk to your career, obviously not for scientific advice since you're a real scientist –
Debug, Zab.
You sent it, I mean, for an obvious reason. You even said I'd understand why when I read it. And I did. And I agree.
But that would only be a wild ass guess.
A wag, a swag even, remember?
I want more than just agreement Zab. You remember more than I do.
But you have the original floppy.
I couldn't quite meet her gaze, nor did she hold it but followed mine out of the terrace-door towards the monstrous euroglobe and the distant hills beyond.
Do I? I said, pretending surprise. Nonsense, Zab, I erased it. You asked me to. Almost ordered me.
She ignored this.
Okay Jip, let's analyse the situation and consider the possibilities.
The sitrep's done that.
Yes, but in such technical jargon the whole thing gets blurred.
That from you?
It wasn't the jargon itself that bothered me Jip, obviously, but the way it was used to neutralise and disguise dismay, indecision, incomprehension, fear (the list impressed me, she always did have the gab for moral issues). I think we should go over the facts, one by one, in the light of what you and I know, first the isolated instances, noting down place, time, duration, in chronological order, then as they get more complex, rediagramming their convergence.
I repeat, the report does just that, in its own technical way.
That's why I said re.

And now all the journalists are onto it and trying to do the same.
    Are they? Already?
    Yes, everything's got suddenly worse in the last few weeks. Overtaken the report in fact, and there've been weekly ones since. Everyone in the world is complaining of long breaks in transmission in both radio and TV, in telexes and telegrams, affecting words and music now, indifferently, and fax, even telephone systems –
    Telephones! Why, of course, they're all on microwave channels now.
    And since international computer systems are linked by phone you can imagine the threatened chaos, something had to give, various statements had to be made by various authorities, and so that's why I came to see you.
    Thank you. But you and I had early experience of reassuring statements to the press by politicians and scientists. In any case, I imagine everyone's investigating according to their lights. Which, however supercompetent, can't include what we know.
    Oh, someone will remember sooner or later. The scientists weren't quite as stupid as we made them out in the Xorandor affair, you know, we were just kids. Some are still studying it.
    She looked at me oddly. I'd forgotten that uncanny quick-connect of hers.
    Okay, she said (VERY archly), so why come to me? Go to them.
    Descramble, Zab. You were full of ideas at the time, some of which I didn't quite grasp then. You were on your philosophic trip already. But we shared something unique. You're my twin.
    There was a longish pause. It was as if she were deciding whether she could forgive me or not, after all this time, whether she could trust me at all.
    Sorry, debugging, she said at last with her old grin. But you're the one who's against tec-recap, so I don't really see what you want. I can't give you a summary reaction as an entity, a kind of maxint label (she was lapsing more and more

into our old language, a good sign I thought) that covers the whole thing neatly like a customs sticker on a parcel. If it's a wag you have, let's treat it as such, a wag's a theory after all, let's go through it like a long equation.

That'll hardly be necessary.

It was a metaphor. Talk, as a butterfly-net, if you prefer. Remember? Even you had to admit that our chatter was a kind of data-network that caught sudden glimpses of ideas.

Okay, but quickly then. It seems to have started with isolated incidents. Planes colliding in mid-air or crash-landing, well above averagewise. At first in Europe, then in America, then in Russia, Canada, Australia. But no one made any connection with anything beyond the usual technical fault, pilot error, or sabotage. I mean anything over and above those, but willed by someone or something, not just chance. No survivors, or at any rate no pilot survivors. But all inquiries revealed one element in common, though this was not made public: in each case the black box and ground sources showed sudden loss of radio-contact. No, sorry, at first Ground could hear the pilot but he couldn't hear Ground. Later both were getting lost. Radar was sometimes okay, sometimes haywire. That lasted over a year, on and off. No recognisable pattern, as you saw from the graphs. Then suddenly it stopped. At least those studying it went on expecting crashes but they never came. Meanwhile pilots had worked out a hypereconomic way of communicating, in case of cut-off.

Cause and effect? Zab asked. I guessed what she meant but pretended not to, as indication that I didn't want to bring in, just yet, any conceivable force that could be supposed to have a will, to be exercising judgment about anything such as economy of communication. She shrugged as I went on.

So it had started on the very low frequencies. After several months, broadcasts started going off the air suddenly and coming back, also on Long Wave. This happens so often anyway no one thought it abnormal or made the connection with the planes. But when it increased well beyond the norm, in all metre-bands, and affected TV, and radio-stations all over the world started sending in requests to Nasa to investigate over and above what they themselves could do in their own technical capacities – which for major stations are considerable – the connection was made and studies were ordered.

Those summarised in the report? There seemed to be no particular pattern. Shall we screen them again and see what we can do together?

You mean you kept the diskette I sent you? I asked you to erase.

She shot me a sharp look, but didn't take up.

Well yes, suitably camouflaged as something else. I transferred different elements to the middle of other files, with callcodes recognisable only by me.

Which you'll forget.

No, I have them down but reencoded three times.

Leaping leptons! I didn't ask you to memorise or keep access to all the technical detail but to give me a reaction.

Which you'd at once say was unscientific unless it arose directly out of the technical detail.

Oh stubs, Zab, let's get on with it.

Okay. I want to get back to the planes for a picosecond. It said Europe, America, Russia, Canada and Australia. Do you know what countries in Europe, what countries in America?

Britain, France, Germany, Switzerland, the USA.

The very countries that had Alphaguys. Britain, France, Germany and Russia first, then Switzerland, Canada and Australia got later offspring. Odd coincidence.

But who gave them up. All seventeen offspring were sent back to Mars with Xorandor.

Except the two he told us to hide, remember. Which he named Uther Pendragon and Aurelius, after that first story of Pennybig. She died, you know.

I nodded, scared of her sidetracking. But she was reacting as I had hoped, and luckily it wasn't a real sidetrack.

And when we got back from Germany they'd disappeared, remember? All offspring had to move while still small enough to be sent like a nodule onto some moving vehicle. That's how they displaced themselves, and spread.

She seemed to go off into a daydream. To encourage her

back I went on: And then of course there was no verification procedure after Xorandor and his seventeen offspring were sent to Mars. Each country gave up the number it was known to possess. But by the time the next Mars probe was ready all the offspring could have grown almost to Xorandor's size and reproduced, on the massive radiation intake they were willy-nilly having, compared to the natural radiation of earlier times and Xorandor's own much slower growth. And in twenty-two years any new offspring kept back secretly could have had more offspring. All that, however, is one bit of the hypothesis, and still makes a relatively small number.

Yes Jip, that's where I agree with you. For although you said they were sent BACK to Mars, as everyone thought, you're thinking of Xorandor's alternative story of their origins, the one he gave us right at the end, and to us only, and which we didn't know whether to believe or not, and had no means of checking. That their race of silicon-based computerstones have been here since the beginning of time, long before man, developing on natural radiation, and moving as best they could, on scaly animals perhaps. Then on riders' shields and chariots and ships and gun-carriages and trucks and trains and planes and things like that. And listening to mankind for aeons. And more and more so with the development of artificial nuclear energy and the modern outburst of discourse over the waves.

Okay, simmer down. (But I was glad to be reminded of the details). What's always triggered me about that, though, is that nobody has ever found one. After all, Xorandor, who in this version of his story was a mere youngster of four thousand five hundred and odd years, was big enough for us to sit on him.

But unaware that we were, till he contacted us on Poccom. Lots and lots of other people could have seen or even sat on similar stones and –

Before, yes, but not after the hooha, hexadex, it hit world headlines. Everyone would have looked – and they did, not just people but governments, geological teams and such, remember, in all stony areas and deserts and near all nuclear dumps and stations. No one found anything.

She looked thoughtful for a moment.

It is odd, she admitted, at least for the ones that are supposed to have been there since before man, they'd be enormous. Though Xorandor never said that. (She perked up). Maybe his size was maximum, or even abnormal, due to extra and perhaps wrong intake, it was never clear how long he'd been taking Caesium 137 after all. In fact – her face suddenly had its diodic expression. But there was a long pause, when she seemed to be working something out, or maybe hesitating about whether to tell me. When she spoke it was slowly. I wonder, I mean, on the hypothesis, that Xorandor's, second story is true, whether, they couldn't, have developed, even very long ago, a much more, economical, microshape you know, the way our computers got smaller and smaller? After all they were way ahead of our computers then, Xorandor could simulate a reality and decide when a different version was required, just like our FSM computers for instance, today. He even created a computer virus, though inadvertently perhaps.

Zab! that's gigavolt! So they could be quite tiny, indistinguishable from, say, pebbles, the way Uther and Aurelius were when we handled them.

Well, perhaps not quite so tiny. But like the Xors after a few months, say. Remember dad and Biggleton thought offspring were peripherals, to save storage space, each one its own filing system. Cos even if he did have three-dimensional circuits, a stone is nevertheless finite. But Xorandor said no, each one was a complete computer with inherited data, and grew on nuclear energy to store more, though also discarding lots. Perhaps they did learn the division of labour.

So there'd be millions of them by now? And all tiny, Xorandor being an aberration?

And perhaps the older ones were in fact fewer than he thought, or we thought, and stony deserts are very, very big.

I was impressed, though I could think of several scientific objections, notably from the geologists, who know and scrutinise the world's stone-formations pretty well. But I wanted to pursue the theory.

That would be the strong hypothesis as to the possible cause: the alphaguys. Who've been here all the time, whereas the politicians and the few physicists (and as far as I remember no one else) who had access to them, thought Xorandor was unique and that they'd sent him and all his offspring back to Mars, when they started eating warheads.

Yes Jip. That was the reason I asked you to delete the whole thing, so that no one would ever discover this possibly true alternative. We WANTED them, if they existed, to go on eating warheads, without anyone knowing.

She wasn't looking at me but staring again at the Hotair Bubble and the distant hills beyond. It was irrelevant to the argument, why was she harping on it? Especially since I'd been right to keep it, and she wrong to erase it, for it would now be useful to have access to that text. Still, I couldn't help putting a quite other retro-justification:

Well, since no missiles have been used or tested all these twenty years or so of negotiations, we'll never know whether any of those not dismantled were neutralised by the alphaguys or not. If we could know that they were, it would prove Xorandor's second story.

She shrugged. I went on:

Okay, the present trouble is being caused by the alphaguys that have always been there, in that hypothesis. But why? There'd be no reason. They don't feed on electromagnetic waves but on nuclear radiation. That's the reason I need your help. And why planes anyway?

That seems to have been only a beginning. Perhaps they were experimenting. Or else a dramatised warning. The real objective must surely be the media.

But plane-crashes and collisions feed the media.

Precisely. The media collect catas-tropheys.

I smiled dutifully.

But Zab, the cause of these accidents doesn't come out till months or even years later. And the results come nowhere near this hypothesis. And the media forget, it's a tiny item, no one takes any notice. A report isn't drama.

They may have found that silencing the communication of

planes didn't achieve their purpose.

What purpose? You always were offline anthropomorphic about Xorandor, Zab, you can't attribute a purpose to them.

A life-force, then, a survival-kit, call it what you like. You know, I'm stack sure that if all the radios in the world researched way back into all their technical hitches, way beyond the supposed beginning I mean, when they started thinking that the frequency and duration of these hitches were abnormal, they'd find a definite pattern, tho it might be hard to discover. I mean, nobody takes much notice of a break in transmission of say twenty minutes in South Wales, or even New South Wales, later apologised for with some sort of phrase like trouble at our local transmitter or disturbances in the ionosphere.

And you mean to imply that this would suit their supposed purpose?

Even a whole night of planned silence causes no surprise, it's announced in advance, work at the transmitter etc. I used to say, they're cleaning the wave-length, remember?

Are you trying to say it didn't start with planes but already with radio-stations, and much earlier?

Yes. If we bear the possibility in mind when we re-examine the incidences – assuming you have access to all that dataheap, or authority to request its terminal display – we'd find, YOU'd find if you don't want me in on it, that it started long before the planes but no one noticed. The planes would have been only a, kind of, jump-instruction if you see what I mean, which would be why it was given up. I speak in the passive to make it impersonal since you don't like the idea of purpose. But I repeat, these creatures are highly sophisticated computers, STILL more sophisticated than any artificial intelligence we've produced so far, even since the hooha. For instance, for some time now we've had computers than can produce computers, and computers that can diagnose trouble in other computers at a distance: well, Xorandor could do both. As to purpose, even natural phenomena result from incredibly complex but impersonal calculation, think of DNA, so if you prefer calculation to purpose it's okay by me.

All right, all right, dump that.

Fine, I'll stick to my terminology. Maybe the alphaguys didn't "know" yet, or "forgot" (she had the scare-quotes in her voice) that men are so slow with inquiries. After all, what is happening now has nothing more to do with planes, but all to do with media. Yet both are Communication.

But why, Zab?

I suppose you mean cause not purpose. WHY-purpose is perhaps more my Fach, my data-network, WHY-cause, let's call it HOW, is more yours. But we should both think about both, I'm sure they're connected.

She was as sharp, but also as generous, as ever. She'd guessed what I was after. She knew I hadn't kept my promise, that I'd cheated on her – obviously she knew since she'd erased the floppy, cheated back – and that I therefore needed her. She had lived our adventure more intensely, I think, than I did, at any rate she's remembered it in much more detail. And it's that memory, that detail, that I need. And her quickconnect. She said nothing, no real reproaches, and offered her instincts in free collaboration, but only if I wanted it, and with no bargaining. I was quite moved suddenly and murmured: Smart terminal, Zab.

Flipflop, she replied nano. And there are the implications, or eventual results, which go with the WHY. And what to do about it or how to stop it, which goes with the HOW. The why and the whither are my Fach, the hows are your Fach, how it's done and how it can be undone. Have a drink on it.

Good idea.

But after all, Jip, she chattered on obsessively as she served drinks, when a person's talking into a mike they've no means of knowing that they're not being heard, until the tecman tells them – usually quite pico in fact, but meanwhile they go buffering on, and then apologise. And if the trouble's just local the apology merely comes after the program. Still, someone notices, and if it's been going on a long time, overaveragewise, surely the tecmen would have investigated, got together with other stations all over the world and so on.

They have, of course, Nasa for one. In the report. And all

the international broadcasting orgs, in Montevideo for the Americas, in Geneva for Europe, in Budapest (which replaced Prague), in Markala and Cairo, in Tokyo, the lot. And as I said many scientists and even the journalists are on it.

Yes Jip, but not as early as they should have been.

In your supposition. Is it so important?

It may be wrong. I just hoped we could go back much further than they have. Or perhaps they have, some of them. But perhaps after all it hardly matters now. It would have been interesting to discover a larger pattern – did it start as suddenly and arbitrarily, here and there, as it seems from that report? And where, and how long each time? And so on. It might also give us a clue about the WHY. Which messages for instance. This would be easier to establish when there were still few cuts. It might even tell us something about the HOW. After all, when messages are intercepted by an enemy, they still reach their destination, and the receiver can't know that they've been intercepted, except from other sources. Same with documents microfilmed on a space the size of a microdot. Not at all like the missives people used to hide in cleft sticks or vaginas. Here, however, it IS like messages stolen from cleft sticks, they don't reach their destination, people do know they're not receiving. The words broadcast don't arrive, they disappear.

Eaten up.

By logophagoi.

Yes, by logophagoi. Much better than Speakloss or even Verbivore.

Oh, I don't know, Jip, I like Speakloss too. It marks what's been happening anyway. Just watch anyone really speaking off the cuff. Even highly educated politicians or scholars, rarely get to the end of their sentences coherently. Look, here's a sentence from a scholar on some B.B.C. cultural program I heard, I jotted it down: *Here a constituent of oral performance enters into a later form, and in so doing we can come to understand how a text is multitemporal.*

What's wrong with it, apart from incomprehensible jargon?

You too! Nor can people listen to the end. That's why radio

discussions have to be broken every few minutes with discs, and TV ones with publicity, for different reasons but with the same effect. That started way back, before we were born, some U.S. president, Nixon I think, organised his election campaign in flash snippets because, he said, the average voter can't concentrate more than three minutes without wanting a beer. Now we weren't like that, but even twenty years ago we were considered whizz-kids, just because we could understand computers, which all kids do today. But something else has gone, which we had, a sort of general literacy, and curiosity, perhaps because we had every advantage, not in money but in our parents, a scientist father, a literary and theatrical mother.

You're talking like a teacher, Zab. Dad was strict with us, but he used to say HIS teachers complained of illiterate students and no doubt so did THEIR teachers. But if it were so we'd have no one capable of putting two words together by now, or of running anything.

Precisely.

Gigo. Language changes, that's all, it's the only truly democratic institution in the world, the people always win against the academicians. Look at the funny, unacademic words the scientists keep inventing. And the best students all learn their speciality soon enough.

And become Fachidioten, as Dipling already said dad was.

Who?

Herr Groenetz.

You really have become impossibly isolated, Zab. Some sort of intelligent elite will always have to run things, even if eighty percent of those are relatively mediocre, and this whatever the political system and whatever the transmission media. As long as everyone's given their chance at the start, the others have to make do in the world as they've made it. You probably only come across those, in Parliament, or when you taught. But there are lots of highly intelligent people in all branches of knowledge. Let's get on with our hypothesis for swag's sake.

Twenty-two years is a long time for human memory these

days. Almost a quarter of a century of eproms and eroms and volatile memories and dynamic memories and parallel memories and serial memories and so on. All memory is on file, all counting and all logical operations are inside a software. You noticed, no doubt, that the report doesn't even touch on the possibility of alphaguys as cause. All is imputed either to some mysterious new air-pollution, that's not only irreversibly destroying the vegetation and the ozone layer as we've known and done nothing about but talk for forty years, but hypothetically damaging the ionosphere or even somehow the wave-lengths themselves. Or else to the ENEMY, whoever that may be in these days of presumed total disarmament.

There's always an evil empire in every government's policy, it's necessary to stay in power or get it.

I may be pessimistic, Jip, but you're downright cynical.

It's all one to me. As far as morals are concerned I see no difference between a political enemy and pollution of the planet, which is the enemy within, no projected scapegoat possible there. But in physics and chemistry we do have to distinguish. To get back to our problem, the report doesn't decide between words and waves. Is this enemy, if there is one, intercepting and eating up the words we broadcast or the supports we generate in order to broadcast them?

Destroying a wave-length for a time-length? Besides, waves, particles, words, all the same, all energy, all physical.

Metaphor and over-simplification won't help, Zab. I meant –

I wonder why it doesn't. Decide, I mean. Surely the processes can be very precisely monitored.

They are. But, well, you know what rival theories are. What I meant was, is this so-called enemy eating up words or, as one theory goes, absorbing radio-waves, consuming, say, all the negentropy by feeding on the bumps, the modulations in the signals which are used to code the information? Flattening out the wave –

Eating up, absorbing, consuming, feeding on, you sure use meta – Jip! I've just had a megavolt brainwave.

Macrosuperdiodic, yes?

Don't tease. It's nice to retrograde with you.

I WAS retrograding with you, not teasing.

I beamed at her because I felt she was moving in my direction and going to suggest what I wanted her to suggest. She went much further.

Supposing, she whispered excitedly, her eyes shining, supposing we could contact Uther or Aurelius? They must also have encoded that secret number Xorandor gave us to get through to Xor 7's oldest memory. All his offspring automatically received all his data.

But (I must say I was astonished), but hadn't he already asked us to take them away, long before the hooha, when he gave us this number?

Can't remember. Look it up, Jip.

She looked away at the giant bubble and hills again. Was she teasing? Telling me she knew I hadn't erased it, but not that she had? As she must have. Or could it have been dad? But why? He'd surely have needed it, for his own book. Which didn't use our data. She went on, with only an imperceptible pause, while these questions flashed through my software:

But they weren't far away, at first, they could have listened in. And my memory of Xorandor's explanation about his offspring is that they were programmed with everything he was programmed with, at birth, I mean all the logical circuits and addresses and essential data.

Of course we've no idea when they moved, or where.

We divided that number in two and each of us memorised half of it, it was so long. I still remember my half, I kept saying it like a poem learnt by heart. D'you remember yours?

Stubs, no, Zab, what d'you expect: We were thirteen, that's twenty-three years ago! But do you mean we could call them up, or one of them, on a computer, and they'd answer, from wherever they are, and EXPLAIN ALL? (Caps meant to be heard in my intonation).

It might have been worth a try.

I very much doubt it. You were always sentimental about Xorandor, but he didn't function on feeling, and nor would his offspring. He wasn't a science-fiction computer, which always has a human weakness somewhere.

No, he functioned on memory. And he did have a weakness, if only for Caesium 137. And it seems to me we did pretty well getting through to Xor 7 with that secret access number.

AND our voice identities, remember. They were like DNA fingerprints to Xor 7. Our voices have changed, even yours has got deeper since you were thirteen.

But we wouldn't use vocal now, how could we? Besides, it'd be intercepted. Remember the voice thing was purely accessory, a provisional technical development for Xorandor's purpose.

Purpose again! Hmmm. Quite a thought, though. Edge-triggering in fact. I'm almost sure we never gave the number in the narrative, so "looking up", if we could, would be pointless. (Our glances crossed again and veered off). I wonder if I can somehow recall my half-number if I try hard? Or maybe if I don't try, if I order my brain to look for it and then just go on doing other things. Say, Zab, do you still have Poccom 3?

She hesitated for a fraction of a second, or was she trying to remember?

Swipes, no. I did keep it for quite a time in the attic junk, but then it became Hanjo's room and I cleared everything out. Now it's my teleport. But in any case it wouldn't be much use as a computer these days. Oh, Jip! You're hexadex right! We encoded that number in SOFTKEY! Screwbooles for sentiment, eh? In fact it wasn't sentiment that made me keep it. When you went to Cambridge and I came to Aachen, I simply didn't want to leave it in Cornwall where dad could get at it. Remember? He was writing a book on Xorandor and knew far less than we did, except I mean as a physicist, and we wanted to keep it all to ourselves.

(That of course was a splendid lie, since she had already erased the whole story from my hidden floppy, nor did it tally with our official version that I had erased it as asked. A lie to deny sentiment). I merely said, gently: That's a feeling too, Zab, it's called possessiveness.

If you like. But you felt it too, Jip, you know you did, dad was such a mental monitor at the time.

And aren't you glad? He taught us rigour.

Yes, of course. Poor old dad, he died so soon after. We were rather mean, we should have helped him write a really good book, our secret knowledge plus his superior physics and rigour. But he probably wouldn't have believed we had other knowledge than his. He never even saw his book come out. I've always been certain his cancer was caused by the nukewaste they were storing down that old tin mine at the Wheal.

Nonsense, Zab, it's –

Oh, don't give me the professional physicist's reply, Jip. How absolutely bootloading that I didn't keep that Poccom 3. How long are you here for?

Not long, we're going on to Austria and Italy, picking up a car on Tuesday. You're invited to dinner at the hotel by the way, I forgot to say. I didn't expect you to cook for six.

Oh? I wish you hadn't forgotten. I've got everything ready-to-serve but cold, we can sit on the terrace, it'd be hopeless in the kitchen or on this small table here.

Oh, well in that case, thanks, I'll give Jeanie a ring. But come tomorrow night. And meanwhile look for Poccom 3, just in case you did keep it after all, and let me know if you find it, I'll come right over.

But the next day, Zab called from her teleport. Not because she'd found Poccom 3 but because she wanted me to see the text of some ancient quarrel she'd had with old Herr Groenetz in Bayreuth at thirteen or fourteen years old! Dipling, as she called him. She wanted to know if I'd heard about it at the time, or if Frieda had told me the next day. Real Quatsch. As if I could remember things like that. The joke is that she can't remember it either, not one word, and even wonders whether she invented it. That's what seemed to random-jitter her most, that memory-blank, that dependence on an old floppy that might have got dumped. That might as well have got dumped. I told her Herr Groenetz was pushing seventy even then, he was much older than Frieda, he'd married her at 55 or more, and Rudi was at least 15 when we went there. So that he must almost certainly be dead now. That seemed to shake her, but also to interest her in some morbid way. If he was nearly seventy at that time, she said, then he would've – but she clammed up.

What I find extraordinary is this idea of rushing home to type up a quarrel into the computer while it's still "wortwörtlich". Real spiky that, she always was an oddboole kid. But then, what am I doing now? Not that it's a quarrel, though it might have been, at several moments, if our old telepath hadn't after all helped us to avoid ever making anything explicit, surging up to function all the same, quite subtly, when I thought it was dead for ever. But she is difficult. She's become cranky and isolated, alone in her little roof flat, thinking she has all the moral answers and unaware of the sheer sophistication and efficiency of modern power organisations, of all sorts, scientific, mediatic or political. For let's face it, the European Parliament is hardly a modern power organisation, more of a cumbersome and anachronistic joke, however seriously it takes itself. Her micropolitics seem to have microcosmified her software. Still, one needs cranks at times, and her memory of the Xorandor affair is stupendous. I've forgotten so much of the detail, but then, I have been involved in so many equally and even more exciting things at Nasa, and kept so very busy, I never gave X another thought. I wish I'd taken that floppy with me to hospital and not been rushed off so urgently in acute pain. I'd still have access to it and wouldn't have to tap Zab. Though she does have these diodic brainwaves.

At any rate, my entering this dialogue isn't at all the same thing as entering a quarrel. I learnt very early, during the Xorandor episode in fact, never to trust my memory of anything said, or seen, or experimented, nor to trust anyone else's, and to record every important conv, either on tape at the time, or wortwörtlich fresh and at once, pico. It's not quite as rigorous as the notes of an experiment, but then nor is conversation. And dialogue's dead easy, I just let the voices on the tape speak, adding minimal stuff about thoughts and looks. As we did for Xorandor, no commentary-Quatsch – well, Zab had plenty, she always did intervene too much. Trap, that's also what I'm doing now, I wonder why. Guilt, I suppose, chattering soothes it away. But who knows, if all this peculiar subroutine on the radio-waves is going to spread further than the present strobing, we may not be able to record or transmit sound electronically any more. Might as well be in good memory-training for the wortwörtlich.

6

Popped over to see mum in London before leaving for European trip, as we'd landed in Aachen New International Airport. Pleased to see us, tho kids push her mentally upwards towards old age. So Jeanie says but I think mum's saner than most actresses about age, she revels in it rather, she started so late after all, leaping straight into stardom when pushing forty, from betrayed wives to tragic queens without ever a single soubrette or juvenile lead, she proudly declares.

Took her out to a quiet dinner alone after *Hamlet* (she played Queen Gertrude) and managed to slip in a casual-sounding question about our childhood tapes. Just testing hypo that it was dad who ferreted in my physics papers and effaced X. Highly unlikely, but one never knows. Not her age she doesn't want to be reminded of, however, but dad and her pre-stage life. Sometimes I wonder how she brought us in and up at all.

Tried to explain a bit about radio-cuts as she was still upset about some role she'd played – oh yes, Lady Macbeth, how funny – having been wiped out and never put on again. She'd written to Tim about it, quite formally, and got no reply, imagine. He's now running the B.B.C., what a career, I suppose his role in Xorandor got him noticed. Doubt whether she understood. As inconsequential and full of quotes as ever.

Negentropy! Is that what Jip said? I wish I'd listened more carefully. Or listened more when John was still studying physics and trying to share his enthusiasms with me. But then I'd have forgotten most of it anyway by now. And here I am trying to write things down, I have nothing to fill my time with, yesterday was the Last Night and I'm "resting" as we say, but a bit alarmed as nothing much else is on the horizon, I'd had a whole series of broadcast performances booked, both TV and radio, but they've cancelled everything "provisionally".

The negative of entropy I suppose, Second Law and all that, I do remember the litcrits grabbing at that because of something someone had said half a century before about their ignorance. That and the Principle of Uncertainty, hardly a writer who didn't have to show he'd heard of them and drag them in at the drop of a thinking cap. John used to say they misapplied the concepts right and left. And just as entropy is always increasing, so negentropy is for ever decreasing, he said, Jip I mean. In the universe at large as well as in local systems. What a depressing thought. Perhaps that's why – no I'm getting confused. How can negentropy, if it means information, be for ever decreasing when all the media are for ever raising information to the nth power?

Well, yes, I did ask him that, and he said that's just the point. Information in the scientific sense. I only ask for information I said. I wish I understood. I ought to, working sometimes in radio-plays, but do actors in front of a mike, or even radio-producers, have to understand radio-waves any more than editors and publishers or even writers have to understand the neurological process of writing? And it is neurological, I can almost feel the thoughts going down through my arm and fingers and pen onto the paper, it's a strain because I'm not used to it but it's a marvellous feeling. Can't think why writers all sit at a keyboard and screen these days, and call themselves wordprocessors. Where was I? Oh yes, both writing and broadcasting are a silent process, because radio-waves make no sound, Jip said, they can even travel in vacuo, the signal's detected as sound only when it activates a receiver. That much I understood. Just like thought in fact, detected only when it hits a vocal cord or a stone, a parchment, a piece of paper, a screen. Stone to screen. That clangs a brainwavelength somewhere. Inestimable stones, unvalued jewels. All scattered in the bottom of the sea. Some lay in dead men's skulls. Maybe Jip and Zab are onto something.

But surely the scientists know what's happening, technically speaking (or not speaking)? As one theory goes, Jip said, so they must have been studying it all very carefully. But can one examine radio-waves to see if the bumps have been levelled out or eaten up or whatever? Surely one can only work it out from effects? And what does it mean, eating, absorbing, feeding on? And wouldn't the creatures, if any, have to excrete? I can't remember how that turned out in the Xorandor episode, after all, they WERE eating isotopes or something. But I never paid much attention to all that. I was rather unhappy in those days.

Well, there's no point in my breaking my brains on that aspect, presumably the technicians and the powers that be will resolve it and explain it all simply, vulgarise it as Zab says the French say, which she says shows how elitist their system still is. I always used to say simplemented, which made John laugh. But it's tempting to ring up Tim and ask him what he thinks. He owes me a letter after all. And I've learnt just enough from Jip not to seem too ignorant. I do understand things providing they're explained to me three times, and it's rather embarrassing to ask the same person.

No, she won't ring Tim, she's too proud, after all she wrote to the D.G. and never got a reply, then to Tim and ditto, and women of her generation, especially actresses who live in other worlds, never forgive a discourtesy. And she never really liked him anyway. But why am I writing all this out as if I were trying to assimilate myself to her? Are these increasing breaks in our daily fictions turning us all into d.i.y. fiction producers? Which, Zab would cut in, we've all been all along anyway, but in our heads, not on paper. I know, she'll run into Perry Striker, or whatever he calls himself now.

Perry darling! Ages. Why don't you write me a play, with a superpart for an aging Dame? No one writes those any more.

Paula, you were a marvellous Gertrude. I will. But you must fire me with your sublime. What sort of part? Harrowed heroine or hideous hag?

You wouldn't even ask the question if the British Government, typically at the time I'm convinced, hadn't thought up

DAME as fair equivalent to SIR for knighthoods, because LADY was reserved for wives of knights or lords and daughters of dukes.
 But Paula, DAME is only LADY in French.
 Yes but think of the degradation since the middle ages and its romantic imitations. I sometimes feel like a man in a pantomime. And don't say no darling you look like La Belle Dame sans Merci.
 I wasn't going to. I may have the germ of an idea, though.
 Oh.
 What enthusiasm.
 Well, I've noticed it's always bad writers who talk about the germ of an idea.
 If you think that, I'll write it for someone else.
 Blackmail. As if playwrights had power. It's the director who does all the writing these days, he even invents the scenes and dialogues as he goes.
 Yes. ZABAGLIONE'S HAMLET with William Shakespeare in tiny letters. But you're right. Even a radio-producer takes over our scripts and fades whole speeches in and out and we're not even welcome at rehearsals. I tried to write that into one of mine – maybe you heard it, A ROUND OF SILENCE (Silence). Well anyway, it was cut long before it got to that bit. All this Logfag thing you know.
 Yes, what is it? Same happened to me in the middle of my sleep-walking scene. What's going on, Perry?
 People interfering with the wave-lengths, they say.
 My son, who's a physicist, said it had something to do with Negativity. Or was it Relativity? No, that wasn't it either. Neg something. Oh I know, negentropy. The negative of entropy you know. Continuous loss of information, he said.
 But, but, what does that mean, continuous loss? You mean it's a natural process? I thought it was entropy that was continuous loss, and of energy. I thought these interruptions were due to specific agencies of some sort, you know, like pollution of the ionosphere or something.
 Yes, well, I've forgotten what he said, and didn't exactly grasp it anyway. But Perry, if we're going to be deprived of

all electronic media in this way, whatever the cause, just imagine, there'll be a rush back to the theatre, the old-fashioned theatre on boards, before 800 to 1,000 people. Or is this going to affect all sound? I mean are the sound-waves being eaten up too?
Poor Decibel.
Who?
Makes no sense, Paula, how could we be talking?
Perhaps we're not, perhaps we're only being written. Or perhaps we'll all be reduced to whispering straight into each others' ears.
Or to silence.
Intolerable. But they'll need us, Perry, they'll need writers again and actors with memories.
For lines learnt by heart.
My daughter used to say that humankind has lost its memory, what with computers registering everything and even newscasters incapable of utterance without telecues. And all that, you know.
Like old people. The old age of the race.
Not at all. Old people have a tenacious memory for anecdotes from their youth. It's only what's just been said they forget. This is just the other way round.
Other way round to what?
To what I said before. You never listen, Perry, you're so intent on noting people's idiosyncrasies for your next play you don't hear what they say.
I defy you to repeat coherently whatever it was you said before.
My daughter used to say that humankind –
Oh, cut it out. You repeat what your precious kids tell you without understanding it.
Perry, you're being extremely rude. I don't think I'll accept the part after all.
I haven't written it yet. Let alone offered it.
Get out.
Yes darling. See you sometime.
How ill-behaved they all are. When I was a child I was taught

to respect my elders, all of them, whatever their sex. I always gave up my seat to an old man and stood aside for any older person with parcels in a narrow passage or held the door. But nowadays when I'm carrying parcels in a narrow passage, and with my greying hair, I'm the one who stands aside to let a young man or girl in trousers push by without a word of thanks. World upside down. Yet when they come to the stage-door for autographs they still fawn. Not that they do that much these days, it's all for popstars and politicians, people who don't last out a fad or an election. Time is like a fashionable host, that slightly, well, and all that.

How depressing it all is. Negentropy. That was it, negentropy. Real information, for ever decreasing, in all systems and in the universe at large. Sounds very grand, but what does it mean? Information means something new, and there's nothing new under the sun, 99.999% repetition, the Xorandor-stone used to say, it's all been said before. So why do we still need to say things? I must ask Zab when I next see her, she'll have an answer of sorts. No, I'll ring. Though of course that merely proves the basis of the question so I should be able to answer it by analysing why I want to ring her. But I'd rather be told.

Couldn't get through. It rang, several times, then cut off, as if she'd lifted the receiver and replaced it. This went on happening so I gave up. I suppose she's busy. Very selfish of her, though, she might have guessed it was me. Unless it's that Verbivore thing again. But surely they can't get at telephones? I'll have to write. Hate writing letters. Or wait till she rings. Then she'll say she can't answer philosophical questions like that on the telephone. If it is philosophy. Psychology maybe. Or anthropology. Yes, she'll say it's not a philosophical or a political question so beyond her competence. Her Fach, as she calls it. She's barely capable of speaking English any more, without inserting German words I have to have explained. Jip's much more amenable, doesn't mind vulgarising for me, as the French say. What a word, vulgarising, Zab's right, there's nothing more elitist than a left-wing French intellectual, total contradiction in terms, bunch of contradictions in fact. Not that I know any. Why am I scribbling all this to myself after an exhausting Last Night and a tiresome morning scene with a yuppish though middle-aged dramatist? Perhaps I'll send these pages to Zab for comment. I've certainly never kept a journal before, it's not an age of journals. And they're such a bore. Saw W, in fine form, told me that B was marrying A / was standing for Parliament / had started a computer-business / was ruined / was sleeping with M / had said y about me. Dinner at C's. And so on. Seems only politicians, generals and aging literati keep journals. Perhaps everyone will now, it's catching. Once one puts pen to paper it runs away in trivia. But it's soothing. Very soothing.

Perry Hupsos. What a name. Greek origin I suppose, everything in -os is Greek. Except cos. He must think he came out of that one-up, oh well, let him.

I came out one-up. Silly bitch. Thinks because she's a Dame she can yuppity me. What was she on about anyway? Actors are a race apart, tear each other and love each other to pieces, no contact with real people. Not like wordprocessors, we have to understand people. Julian, for instance. I really got inside him. And even Decibel. Yes, I'm a bit in love with Decibel. I wonder whether I'd have killed her off if I'd finished the play. It's because I didn't know that, or how to end, that I stopped with a radio-cut. Joke, supposedly, and the waves took their revenge. Killed her off, since she can't live on silence. Whatever the waves are. Sounds crazy. Sounds no sounds at all.

The silence is terrible, I'm having to take refuge in traffic jams and building-sites and shunting-yards. I used to just sensually swell myself up into existence, floating in and out of homes with the telly on all day or the radio as background noise, wallpaper radio, some insomniacs kept it on all night, sends them to sleep they say, ooh, it was lovely, loud music, from France, England, Spain, and so on and so forth, the inane chatter and false hilarity of falsetto disc-jockeys, and always the same disc-horse, who said that, oh Mira, here she is, but she always preferred droning discussions, vox humana the best sleeping-draught she'd say, still, it was noise after all, and allowed me to detumesce a little yet not die altogether. But what shall I do if the delectable decibel-making media banish me altogether as they seem to be doing? I'll have to live hard for my living. Poor Julian, he hated noise. I had to leave his head. I wonder how he's faring. He must be revelling in the new situation, more than a round of silence, a sphere, a globe, a universe of silence. What bliss. At last I can work, get on with my thesis. But what for? What on? No more posts anywhere, all humanities abolished, all Universities as lean and fit as industrial plants, as lean and fit as they used to be before the twentieth century boom when modern literatures replaced the classics as megavolt grounding for a gentleman, and a natural stepping-stone to the Foreign Office. And then by mid-century, why just gentlemen? Why not women and working-class and all races? The opening to all, the making of thousands and thousands more experts on Joyce or Goethe or Wilberforce or Villiers de l'Isle Adam all fabricating more Joyceans Goetheans Wilberforceans de l'Isle Adamians when no one outside the enclaves reads Joyce Goethe Wilberforce de l'Isle Adam. Just like the Middle Ages when who outside the monasteries read the Eternal Commentary? But it was all still relatively reduced then. Now, databanks and datasinks of analyses, explications, deconstructions, reconstructions, paraconstructions, interpretations and reinterpretations. Quoi de neuf, Sacha Guitry used to ask, and answered: Molière. While outside, the world transformed itself jet-propelled into an earth-sized nuclear power-station and electronic medium. Medium for what? The global village?

Who made me? That old-fashioned idiot Perry Hupsos and his producer Mira Enketei, together they created me and saw that I was good and dead. Nobody like me exists any more, nor like my wife Barbara, let alone that prim pedant Vivien Nicholl. Put another Nicholl in, gigo! So what's to become of me? And where is Decibel? I wonder how she's surviving in this blessed silence. Probably haunts the shunting tracks as she said.

So I'm not at all getting on with my dissertation on neo-postdeconstruction, so useful to society – and everyone has been doing it for years anyway. Research is no fun these days, databanks not for thumbing. Even authors don't send typescripts to publishers any more but one small diskette, that merely gets checked, reprocessed, and multiplied for the market. Second-hand bookshops are rarer and rarer, and quickly close down. No more poring over old books in libraries, or by candlelight as in old paintings, just reading off screens, and with no guarantee that sentences, paras and even chapters haven't been erased for compactness. Libraries are supposed to check every new diskette that comes in, but the task is like emptying rivers with a sieve in fairytales. So errors and misquotes and omissions get perpetuated at an even greater pace than before, scholars being such cheats with quotes and opinions, repeating them wholesale from each other without screening the original. No wonder governments have done away with all that. It's kept only for historians, and they'll probably be eliminated too.

So instead, I've taken to spilling myself out into the wordprocessor like everyone else, to give myself some sort of illusion of existence. Did people really feed on that daily fountain of electromagnetic fictions? Feeding on beings like me, but more so? And now that they're losing us, what will happen to them? Without, if it goes on, their daily ration of savoured suspense, salacious sex, peppered plots, aromatic romance, vapulated violence and chocolate charm? Not to mention the swift computerdaelic designs and unisex unirace singers jerking like automata in multicoloured laserbeams – perhaps the only contribution television has been able to make towards aesthetics for all, even if these have, like music, become as noticeable as home dec after the first novelty has passed. Will the people be satisfied with the blurred stills and bloody balladmongers in the tabloids?

Barbara left me. While I was in hospital. She stopped visiting and when I got out she'd gone, presumably had her baby elsewhere, I don't even know its name so it's as if it didn't exist. Couldn't stand my tantrums about noise. Said I'd become incoherently selfish. Would she prefer me coherently so? I asked. Convinced I had a mistress. Apparently I went on calling for Decibel for ages. Oh well good erasure to both. Women! Not worth the effort one has to make to treat'm fairly, as they keep insisting we don't. And as for babies! Never needed sex anyway. More like Mira Enketei, inside the whale, happier with books and screens, they don't answer back, one reads what one wants into them. Come to think, it's the same with the media I guess, but collective, everyone's like that basically, can't cope with the other's mere existence annulling their private fantasies. That would explain the world's infatuation with media, they fed fantasies. That's how those responsible justify it all, we bring them a moment of happiness. Same with the tabloids, they're giving the public what it wants. Unaware it's the identical argument as that of the drug-pushers. Fell for that in a big way, the world did, right through the twentieth century, more and more like a drug. I'm sure it wasn't quite like that with just books and plays, before the media existed, at least only for a relative few, who were relatively civilised. Culture always acts as a protection against itself, against its own abuse, like homeopathic medicine, tiny doses, or like injections of insulin for the diabetic – also a relative few. Above all not all of the time. But then, everything is called culture these days, beer-drinking, car-driving, living, loving, sailing round the world on a log or growing soya beans.

Perhaps I should write my dissertation on that, and change to Sociology. Oh no, that's a Humanity too, gone with the rest. But I could make it more hitec, with a bit of hard work, and do it in Communications, that's still an okay subject. But probably everyone's on to it. Or maybe, yes, wordprocess a novel about it, much easier, more fun. Perry seems to enjoy it anyway.

I should call Mira, or rather, somehow program her to call me, it's easier for her after all, she produced me. She and Perry. But he's visiting the Soviets under his old pseudo Perry Striker, they'll love that, they always did idolise their dead myths. No, I must concentrate on Mira, force her to think me up.

It doesn't seem to work. Of course she's very busy. Processors who become producers, publishers, editors, reviewers, teachers and other middlemen seem to dry up, even though they've got there by processing in the first place. I'll try the actor who played me, what's his name, they say actors become the character they act. But without the name it's difficult, and I suppose I ceased to exist for him as soon as the play was recorded, he'd become someone else. Oh Mira Enketei help.

Talking of actors, no one has yet commiserated in public with the star-newscasters, who get so addicted to their framed projection and all the feedback idolatry it entails, and the way the rival channels buy them up from each other at higher and higher salaries like football stars. Like that Nigerian on the nine o'clock news, Onuora Nwankwo. They can never quite adapt when they're removed from that for age or image-fatigue or politics or other reasons, even to more important but backroom jobs with a huge drop in salary. They'll suffer from withdrawal symptoms as much as the public will, same with all the presenters of fortune-wheels, pyramids, right prices and variety shows, same with their radio colleagues on their aural pedestals. They're all in love with the projected image of themselves, returned. But then aren't we all? The humbler rest of us merely have to make do with less powerful returns and meagerer means. Means, media, ha! Where is she, inside the whale, the Beehive B.C., come on out, Mira, make contact with me or I perish.

A ROUND OF SILENCE. Yes, that too is due for a repeat. But no point. We should scrap all repeats and concentrate on the new, even if it's only to be cut. Still, policy is to go on as if. Okay then, add it to the list and send it to Scheduling. Perry'll be pleased. And that poor marginal what was his name, John, Jasper, no Julian. In love with Decibel, or tormented by. Hello? Oh, Sir Timothy. Yes sorry, Tim. I know you said so but hierarchy dies hard. Yes I'll come right away.

Ah, Mira, sit down. Did you have any luck?

A bit. I located Zab, she's in Aachen as a Euro-M.P. for Aachen Kreis, the International District. Became German, you know. So she doesn't have to commute like –

Cut the trimmings, Mira.

You sound like Jip during X. Well, he visited her, to discuss a secret Nasa report he'd sent her. But he seemed anxious to get hold of the original diskette of Xorandor, which Zab had asked him to erase, and he hadn't, so she'd copied it and erased his, fine behaviour for loving twins I must say. Anyway there was a certain tension between them. But they were both onto the idea, as obviously you have been, that the descendants of Xorandor are responsible for all this interception, no, this swallowing act. Xorandor was equipped with highly powerful listening devices you remember, he was a mega but micro radiotelescope as well as a computer.

I know. And officially he and his offspring were packed off to Mars.

The known ones, yes. But two were secreted off by the kids, on Xorandor's orders, and had vanished from their lairs when they got back from Germany. Or, in another version apparently given to them by Xorandor himself, millions of creatures like him have been here since the beginning of time.

Ah. I remember there was much speculation about that in scientific circles, and many searches were instituted. Even the stomatolites of Hamlin Bay in Australia were examined. After all they were created by the algae that produced the first oxygen on the planet. But it all came to nothing.

Because people went on thinking in terms of very large stones. Zab's idea was that Xorandor was an aberration, due to huge overdoses of radiation from Tregean Wheal, and that in fact the race had long evolved towards more and more miniaturisation, like our computers in fact, but aeons ago. Which is why no one could find them.

And the overloading of redundancy on the waves would be too much for them? That makes sense. It's getting very difficult for us, after all, and worse for our radio-technicians, not to mention aerospace scientists, astrophysicists and such.

They didn't exactly get to the motivation, though Zab tried hard, but Jip wouldn't hear of these creatures having purposes and reasons. Only interested in the how, in fact Zab divided their task into the why for her and the how for him, how it happened and how to stop it – and that's after all what you're after.

Smart terminal, Zab is. Can't deal with how to stop it without understanding the why. Anything else?

Not much. Oh yes, Zab had a diodic brainwave. To try and find the secret code X had given them to reach Xor 7's most ancient memory –

Why yes, I was there. But they didn't use a code-number. Hold on! I think they pressed the Softkey and –

Right. They'd encoded it secretly into the Softkey, having also memorised half of it each in case something went wrong. It was immensely long. Jip's forgotten his half.

That's it! And every now and then a passage from Macbeth would jump him out of it. Zab had to loop to get him out of that. Then Jip took the risk of pressing Softkey again, which could have annulled the number if the jumping hadn't, but it worked.

Anyway, Jip, or Zab, I forget, seemed to think that if they could find that old toy-computer again –

Poccom 3. Completely outphased.

– and press its Softkey again, somehow they could contact at least one of the two secret offspring, wherever they are.

And their means of motion are pretty considerable, they're the means we use, trucks and planes and submarines etc.

Zab said she'd long thrown Poccom 3 away. I'm pretty sure she was lying though. Strange how that twin-relationship deteriorated.

Still, it's an outside chance. Can you contact her again?

I think we'd better leave them, or her, to do the prelims, which may after all fail. They were both highly mistrustful of all grown-ups and official bods, remember, and may have retained some of that.

Not Jip, surely, he's part of official set-ups.

Yes, you could contact Jip, as equal to equal, you were right, he does work at Nasa. Paula has his private address if you want it. But let Zab be for the moment. I feel sure she'll contact you, Tim, or someone, if she gets anywhere.

Okay. Anything else?

Jip had an explanation about negentropy.

Ah yes, we've been working on that.

What does it mean? A radio-producer doesn't get to learn much about waveguides and waves.

You learnt enough about them, and physics, during the Xorandor episode.

Long time ago, and I was helped. And not radio-waves.

They, whoever, would be absorbing all the modulations in the signal. These are what codes the information.

Paula tried to explain but got it confused. She did ask, though, and I couldn't answer, because it never cropped up in the Xorandor episode: if they consume, don't they have to excrete? Zab used to ask a similar question at thirteen, where does it all go, what they absorb, not the nuclear energy, that was clear, but the information they listened to. One answer was that they simply erased all repetition, which according to Xorandor made up ninety percent or more of what they heard.

That wouldn't explain this new phenomenon, though. But they could in theory excrete it as white noise.

White – ?

Or as waves with no modulations. But no, that would give a pure note signal.

We do get those.

In the ordinary course of things, but not permanently. Whereas white noise would have a low signal-to-noise ratio, I mean there'd be a lot of static. High rubbish content if you prefer.

But neither of these is happening, I mean more than it always did, as you say.

No, just silence.

So, no excretion?

Perhaps they convert white noise into silence.

Is that technically possible?

Not to our knowledge.

Pity. Because high rubbish content and silence are philosophical equivalents, in a way.

Philosophic maybe, but not technical. Well, thank you Mira, contact me when you like if you have any news. And carry on as if.

Very costly isn't it? Paying all these actors, writers, speakers, journalists and technicians when the public can only hear bits and pieces.
That's the policy, business as usual, whatever the crisis.
Very British.
No, Mira, it's the policy everyone's following, all over the world. It's the only way we can examine the phenomenon scientifically.
I see. Sorry. I hadn't grasped that obvious point.
And maybe solve it.

7

Weird old Mira, she sometimes behaves as if I had sprung ready-armed from her head. Comes of having no kids I guess. MEMO 1: Locate Dr John Ivor Paul Manning at Nasa and get private number if poss. If not, ring him at Nasa at 5 p.m. (9 a.m. here) and put him through. MEMO 2: Contact Professor Andrewski at UKAEA and ask him to ring me tomorrow afternoon. MEMO 3: Am taking concentration charts and public sitrep file home (8 p.m.) to work on. Will disconnect phone and won't be in till eleven, say I'm in conference. All signed letters in out-tray urgent.

This crisis is getting me down. Everyone expects me to resolve it as if by technimagic simply because I used to be a microwave expert. But that was twenty years ago. One can't switch to admin and remain an expert for long. They should have appointed a hiflying cultureperson or hiflying business person as usual.

Well, I'd better start from scratch with the world occurrence charts in the light of Mira's news, and try and get a fix. Metaphor of course, interceptors can't be fixed the way emitters can. And it's happening all over the place anyway. I know the B.B.C. picture by heart. Ah, here's the latest IIR report, with graphs and charts, that'll help. Together with the Nasa interims.

No doubt about it. There are new concentration spots, and the greatest are in Southern Germany, Kiev, Nagasaki, some place in Manchuria, how odd, Hong Kong, Dakar and Nevada. Just as the P.M. said, must have the same sources. Britain still relatively spared. Second greatest New York,

Washington, Tokyo, Pretoria, Cairo, Canberra, Zimbabwe, Rio, Warsaw, London, Berlin, Aachen, Paris, Rome, Madrid, Jerusalem. Rio, Buenos Aires, that's all much more expected. But the first lot makes less sense. Southern Germany: not Munich so much as Bayreuth. MEMO: isn't that where the kids were sent to school? Could they have taken one of the secret offspring with them? No, that's nonsense. But the German experiments with their specimen were around there, what was his name, expert in nuclear waste-disposal down saltmines? I forget. And Russia. We don't know where they took theirs. Nevada is near enough L.A. where Andrewski had his specimen, given that it escaped there. But what about Manchuria and Dakar? Well, Dakar's the HQ of the Radio and TV Org of Africa, but that wouldn't explain it, besides, their technical centre's at Markala in Mali. All high industrial zones? Or nuclear stations? Reports don't say. Still, in the other hypothesis they could be anywhere. Then there are the many areas dotted with intermittent cuts, purple for highest down to pink for lowest. Covers practically the entire broadcasting world.

Let's see if all this tallies accurately enough with our Monitoring Service reports. They're so damned detailed one can't see the world for the Telexes, i.e. analysis not so much geographical as syntactical, what sentences are most broken into and where. Made sense at first, especially as some people insist it started with syllable cuts. But we've all been getting these print-outs now for weeks and no clear pattern emerges, only amusement at the occasional misunderstanding by monitors: libeedno satisfaction, here, and God has the face of a man and bowzoom of a booman – must have been a Spaniard talking. The pudding of a man to death. And the inanities: You can't compare animates with real life (a program about film cartoons), and someone going on about a mediaeval relic of Christ's aura. We're way past that. Besides, that would impute a motive to these creatures, as if they disapproved of certain words. If creatures there are.

But the geographical situation tallies, here, p.547, Appendix 4. Yes, no doubt about it. And Appendix 5 shows the spread in time. Not counting the early plane-crashes, it started in Southern Germany, spread to Russia, then to England, then a bit all over the place, then each spot grew and grew, except England and Spain where it seems to have remained stable, can't think why. If it is connected with Xorandor and a "sentimental" attachment then why Spain? Why, for that matter, relatively few cuts, though still cuts, in, say, Peru, or Zambia or India or Saudi Arabia no longer either deserta or felix? Sheer chance of presence or chance of coverage? I mean are they everywhere and choose, or are there limits in their interception ranges? If it were a wholly natural phenomenon would there be quite so much chance as opposed to necessity? And could it all just be due to overloading the networks as so many spokesmen against private stations say?

Tired. Let's glance at the sitreps and take notes. Oh – the usual crap. Why does every member of the public who expresses an opinion have this tone of naive conviction that he or she is the first to express it, the first to see things clearly? Well-informed people never write such letters to institutions, they know every single position's been over-expressed for years, for decades, with only the topical incidents as variants. Dear Sir, I must write to protest against the B.B.C.'s continuous left-wing bias in the discussion last night, no wonder the mystery cutters got to work... Dear News, The B.B.C. as usual has yielded to a right-wing government's pressure in... Dear B.B.C., In the minor matter of Verbivore, if such a phenomena exists, no solution will be found with such redtape and barroquacy. No one seems to have pointed out the excedingly obvious fact that... Dear Media Meddlers, I write to say that I have never felt so much relief in all my life that the hedgemony of the ordurevisual is at last taking a big bashing, for I have never been able to stand... Dear Auntie, what shall I do without you? For years I have... Dear Discussion Point, No one in the discussion yesterday seemed to take the blindest bit of notice of the chairman's main point, in which he seemed secretly to revel in the new situation, where here at last was an opportunity for everyone to start learning to read and write and play and make music on their tiny owns again, which

would recreate our lost culture. When I was a child, my mother
...Dear B.B.C., Why does everyone on your staff, when
discussing Verbivore, seem to think we shall die without you,
stifle without your news, perish without your daily commentary, as if we were all totally incapable of...

This is leading nowhere. But it's the first time I've had a
moment to look at these. Perhaps I should let my keyboard
drift, indeed, that's what everyone seems to be doing anyway,
judging by all these letters, which we encourage in every program, and to which the press is having to give increasing space
under mounting pressure from politicians, writers and other
demadogs to let the people express themselves, however
pompously or incoherently. That's been our policy anyway
for years, with phone-ins, TV-games, request programs,
complaints programs, information about antiques, sex, gardening etc, enquire-within programs and the like. Just type
this number on your minitel and we'll contact you. They
responded like queues for bread or popular soups in the old
days, and indeed in certain areas still.

Strange that I should be comparing the media, which everyone so far has spoken of in terms of drug and withdrawal
symptoms, to basic food, bread and soup. The media were
originally welcomed and developed as a marvellous chance to
share out culture, and we used to do a splendid job there, with
plays, beautiful documentaries on space, the origin of the
planet, ecology, plant and animal life, the underwater world,
dying species, pollution, not to mention lively discussions and
polemic at reasonable levels, yet easy to understand, during
which viewers could phone in their questions. And so on. But
by the end of the century they had all yielded, yes, even we
had yielded, to the Audimetre and the sponsors, and started
handing out anything from cars to dining-room suites or
thalasso-cures for answering questions like the name of a top
star's latest companion or the world high-jump record or the
currency of Haiti, the gourde, true or false? Or for guessing
all the missing letters of a proverb, a title, a person, a thing,
very appropriate, excellent training for guessing missing syllables, words, sentences, paragraphs.

But that's all so abstract, even the prizes remained a dream if not won. A simulated world, like those that computers produce. The population has learnt to live on abstractions and interpretations of the world as presented by a few. Perhaps it always was so, in Greece, in the Middle Ages, in the nineteenth century, and it's now simply increased to the nth power. They have forgotten the smell of sawdust and leather and dung and sweat, the feel of gnarled wood, of a cow's udder, the taste of unchemical tomatoes and wild bilberries, the sight of clear water, the sound of crickets and birdsong. Even the miraculous close-ups of all this on nature-programs or commercials are cool abstractions (NOT hot media as the guy once insisted), training the eye and ear at the expense of other senses, and now their eyes and ears are not only weakening, spoilt from surfeit, passivised, but also deprived, suddenly. Naturally the yearning return to simple physical endeavour in the craze for cross-country, sailing, climbing, tennis and all the rest has partly compensated, but this touches only a tiny minority, despite appearances, the huge rest of the population preferring voyeur enjoyment and queuing bumper to bumper in their computerguided vehicles to go and sit watching panoramic spots through the windscreen. Not that I'm any better, I've always just tinkered with microwave sets in a workshop or sat in an office reading reports and presenting them at meetings. We've become stunted human beings. Loss of senses and muscle through the media, loss of memory and logical capacity through computers. Perhaps the deprived of this earth, who have gone through none of these processes, who have to walk fifty miles through the desert to draw a bucket of water, who have gone on tilling their bit of arid earth with camels or oxen or cows or women pulling the plough, will finally take over as fully-developed beings. When the gradual effect of perhaps total deprivation has altered the so-called civilised populations, turning them into stupefied incompetents in acute media-withdrawal, not to mention the real harddrug addicts, then those with highly trained limbs and senses will inherit the earth.

Here are the news headlines. An India Airlines plane carrying

420 passengers and flying from New Delhi to Auckland has crashed into the Pacific Ocean somewhere off Borneo. There are no survivors. We shall be asking, could the black series of plane-crashes that marked the beginning of Verbivore be starting again. The Prime Minister has arrived in Toronto for the Summit Conference. The industrial action of the Kent railway workers has paralysed the Channel Tunnel and the ferry companies are rubbing their hands. The pound is at a new low. (Crash music). Good evening. (Funeral tone). Could the black series of air catastrophes be due to

Black screen, splattered with white dots and silence, like a universe.

The cut came just before the word Verbivore. Is that significant or just coincidence? The word was predictable since the item repeated the headline. But what would be the point? Everyone knows the word so it can't be censorship – though censorship usually is of items everyone knows. But here I am attributing purpose again, like Zab. I really have become very unscientific.

But Zab's idea really is edge-triggering me. After all I witnessed it all, and I knew her pretty well, better than Jip in some ways. I read all the books and stuff that came out about it at the time, both popular and scientific. It amazed me even then that astrophysicists who'd been scrutinising the universe for generations to find extraterrestrials weren't more excited about X. Or geologists, who'd been combing the planet for ancient rock-formations. Except for those few immediately concerned with nuclear waste-disposal and warheads, or with computers, most scientists looked upon the whole phenomenon as a bit of folklore juiced up by the press and swollen by the media. Some did continue to work on it but with the specimens at first so secretly guarded, and then gone, and everything known published, their work meandered into speculation. And many loonies went on proclaiming cranky theories. At any rate, like everything, when the press and the media lost interest, it vanished in the night of time. And I too lost interest, forgot, put other things first. So much else has happened in the world since, not just in politics, the balance of power actually settling to disarmament and superficial peace, but also in my own domain. And now all my hard work, my ambition, my success, all seem as nothing to what is happening now. Perhaps I should resign.

It seems to be a feature of this high-risk technological society that the people who run it, or different bits of it, are not in fact mentally or legally equipped to cope with the unforeseen. A lady in a HST was dying, a doctor was in the carriage and insisted the train should stop at the unscheduled next station. The driver consulted British Railways who said no. She died. That was only last year, and a tiny example. Simply there was no administrative provision, no operational readiness, for such a case. And is a spaceman technically equipped to know what to do if he enters a black hole? In scifi yes, he "warps" or something, but in real life? Have nuclear station disasters been well dealt with so far? Or chemical disasters? We all start attributing responsibilities to other nations, other institutions. Sovereign states, but states of emergency. Permanently. Despite constant reassurances about total readiness for everything. Well, this was unforeseen, unimaginable, and no one knows what the hexadex to do.

I can just imagine Zab in her attic teleport, dragging out the clumsy Poccom 3 and trying to contact Xor 17 or 18 or however they called them. She'd be very secretive about it, she certainly wouldn't inform Jip. Or any of her Euro-M.P. colleagues. This Euromp lark does seem a romp to her, I've never heard of her making any kind of speech, maiden or matron. Not that one hears much about the European Parliament anyway, except when it tries to impose a Eurolaw on a recalcitrant member. Still, at least it's a bit leaner and fitter, in one capital, than when the whole outfit was scattered over three cities, to please everyone, and tons of documents had to be shunted between them in eighteen languages for twenty-three countries. The change was pointless once everything was properly computerised but now who knows, with telephones and computer networks technically susceptible to Verbivore it was perhaps just as well. I'm drifting. As I said I would, but it leads me nowhere at all. Zab must be neglecting her euroduties to pursue her idea.

SOFTKEY Zip calling Uther Pendragon or Aurelius. Come in please.

Repeat.

Repeat.

Repeat.

Blank screen.

What am I doing wrong? Poccom 3 interfaced with transmitter, okay. Of course anyone can intercept but that's a risk I have to take. Probably they're not within range. After all mere mountains can stop us hearing our favourite stations. Perhaps it's a question of patience. Or timing. Or both. I'll just have to keep trying at different times, day after day, or rather night after night, the traffic is less dense, for weeks, maybe months.

Weeks, months, I haven't heard from Hanjo since he arrived. Ages. He never was one for writing, and maybe he can't ring. Where is he? If only I knew at least that he's all right. Perhaps he's failing in his quest and is too ashamed to tell me I was right, but I don't care two nanos for his quest, or for his father, I just want to know he's alive, and not in any kind of trouble. Rushing off to China like that, as naive tourist, probably trying to get to all sorts of places they don't want tourists to go to, without a word of Chinese, and probably ill-equipped for the widely contrasting climates. Though he said he had everything.

SOFTKEY. Zip calling Uther Pendragon. Come in please.

Softone. Zab calling Hanjo. Come in please, Hanjo darling please.

Uther, means terrible, Pendragon, means head, or chief. And Aurelius, named after – wasn't there an emperor? What if Xorandor didn't program their names into them? No, that's impossible, I remember he recalled the names himself, at once, it was he who chose them, not us. Did they also have a Xor number perhaps? If so, which? Nothing for it, I'll have to look up the episode. But I'm afraid to take out the disc. No one knows I have it, though Jip suspected. Supposing someone called and I somehow mislaid it? Supposing he's set a spy on me?

SOFTKEY. Zip calling Aurelius. Come in please. Zip calling Uther Pendragon, come in please.

Softwarily. Mum calling Hanjo please, please write, wire, send in cleft stick, anything.

8

Dear mum,
  Meant to write earlier but so much hapenned since I saw you in Achen I had no time beside chinese phones are cut all the time tho they say its not china but hapening all over so I didnt try due to verbivore wich has a swell picchure sign here a sort of trapese for mouth with flames for words but swollowed or rather preseded by another mouth but I cant do it on the pc I borrowd wich is american I dont know if they use pictchurs on their computers I have desided to be a jurnalist not a physicist and after all news comes from evrywhere these days and life here is very intresting the pilot who brought me here is a girl well a woman I mean she's a bit older but I'm in love with her and plan to marry her when I get back to Europe I mean she doesnt live here but flies the route often tho now I'm in Shensi we cant meet anymore and calling is hopless so we send disketts from Sian to Beyjing and back and

  I cant send that she'll be furious tho she wasnt too pleased about China anyway to learn I send disketts to Régine and not to her and I never told her I faild my exams I thouhgt spelling wdnt matter in maths and physics so I chose them but it did so she'll guess I'll have to tell her but its all so complicated so what shall I tell her? Whatever I do she'll be anoyed so I dont say and dont write then she complains about that she never understood even about my father that I wanted him to know I exist when I said that she ignord it and went on to somthing else but its very important to me espescialy as she anulls me in evrything.
  Régine says I must improove my stile and spelling if I want to go to jurnalism school tho my teacher in colege said about

stilisation being sterilisation so I'm practising writing down evrything she says it will come from doing it but she always lauhgs at me in the next diksette but after all I can always get one of those computers that corect spelling and put in the comas and stops when I'm not phoning in my reports but thats for after first I must get into a school so I must practise I never coud understand the principal of spelling sometimes its one way in one word and then in a scimilar word its another way. Mum used to harp on about etimology thats the histry of each word but by the time youve learnt the etimology of evry word youd be dead. I think its becos she and uncle Jip were such clever kids she exspects me to be the same but theirs no reason if I dont know who my father was tho he was clever too she says. Perhaps I shd have stayed longer in Beyjing to find out more but I was so sure I'd find his trase in Shensi so here I am.

Sian is a mostly modeern provinsial town in a wide valey (the Wei Ho) with high mountains both north and south that's a good start its very hot and humid despite the mountains but their quite far I gather its very cold in winter their are many ciment factories and electrical equipment and coton textile plants it cd almost be an american town with little chinatowns here and there I find it hard to meet people but I started lessons in chinese from a schoolteacher in exchange for english conversation I dont get on very fast everyones talking about no one can hear the radio anymore not even chinese music or watch TV their cut here too so they miss it tho many people hadnt got it or got used to it like we have for generations so they go on as if it had never existed Wey says its universal evrywhere but its not realy part of there sistem as the papers say so he says I cant read them yet they prefer the village to the global village but all the guvernment work is dislocated and the poeple are cheeting like crazy over evrything but they did that anyway before he says the global village idea was compleetly wrong it was some canadian who thouhgt the media woud unite the whole world with immeedjat news from evrywhere but nothings more provinsial than radio and TV for one thing its all in local lingos and the trend with satelites has been towards more and more of the same instead of evryone waching there neihgbors TV and learning about each other and understanding each other you can only do that by coming to live in each place he says and realy learning what poeple are like just like the old days so the only media that helps that is supersonic planes and thats what Ive desided I want to do even if it takes a lifetime to learn each place when hes not teaching he takes me into the less modern parts and its just like the movies or once into the hills there used to be regular famines which doesnt hapen anymore since even remote arias have become easily axcessible and its all very well irigated.

> Dear mum,
> Would you believe it I'm in Shensi, hope your surprised it was meant to. I met a super new freind she's the pilot I told you about who brouhgt me to Beyjing but always off like you and Sian is as far from Beyjing as Athens from Achen she says or maybe Cambridge from Texas were madly in love I want to marry her I also want to go to jurnalism school when I get back and not to be a physisist so I'm seeing things and practising writing and spelling as you see and learning chinese in exchange for english I hope my money lasts it goes quite far here but I can do odd jobs and its important for me to integrate and not be just a toorist and undesirable yooth to them and I hope to learn enough to look for my father soon I hope your well and dont worry about me love and kisses
>
> Hanjo

For a future *grand reporter*, as the French say, there's not much information about China or Shensi or even Sian, and as to spelling! But hell, he'll learn I suppose if that's what he really wants. At least he's all right, at least it's news. Maybe he'll go far, in his own boolesup way. He says damn all about the Verbivore phenom over there. And I'm stuck.

I think I'll ring up Tim, he's high up at the B.B.C. and knows all about these things, maybe he can help.

Hello, I'd like to speak to Tim Lewis please, can you get me his extension?

Sir Timothy is not available madam, can I have your name?

SIR Timothy? Oh, I had no idea, sorry. He's an old friend. My name's Manning.

I'll put you through.
Long costly silence. Or is it a cut?
Hello, Jip? Tim here.
Not Jip, Tim, it's Zab.
Zab! How extraordinary! Sorry, I was expecting a call from Jip, my secretary just said the call from Manning. But I'm delighted. How are you, Zab?
Hexadex, Tim, it's very important or I wouldn't bother you, I mean, I forgot you were director or something, but now I remember. I still need to see you urgently. Here if possible.
Silence.
I know it sounds hopelessly impertinent and I can't explain on the phone.
Not at all Zab, I think I can guess what –
You can? Oh, Tim, I knew you would, you –
Let's be brief in case we get cut. How urgent, will tomorrow do? It's Saturday and I can get the first plane out.
Macrovolt! It arrives at 9.16, I'll meet you.
You are efficient.
I'm used to meeting delegations. Thank you Tim, I'll be wearing a red cotton coat over a white dress in case you don't –
Can I have your address and number in case something goes wrong? Thanks, registered.
Thank you Tim, I do –
Not a word. See you tomorrow.
Thank God that call wasn't swallowed up. MEMO, unavailable all weekend, going to Aix, phone in memory, to be used only in extreme urgency. No one to be told where I am. Should be back by Monday afternoon, if not, will ring if not cut.
So you see, Tim, I felt you might just be able to help me, you used to be such a wave-expert, and you remember Poccom 3, and interfaced it with the IBM for the Xor 7 hooha at Berkeley 2. Maybe it's not working properly any more, but I'm sure I have the right inkling.
Or was it Jip's? He came to see you, didn't he?
How the hex do you know that? Did he tell you?
No, I haven't seen him yet. But I guessed he might.

So you automatically suppose any right inkling must be his?

Sorry, simmer down Zab, I simply assumed, first, that you were the type of person who would have kept Poccom 3, for nostalgic reasons, and secondly, that he might just have had the same idea and tried to get that fact out of you.

Right on both counts. But, well, I'm afraid I lied to him.

You wanted to do it all on your own?

Not out of selfishness, Tim, or ambition, or anything like that. Oh, it's too complicated to explain.

I think I understand, Zab. He erased Xorandor.

No! He promised to and didn't! I discovered that by chance and was so hurt I copied it and then erased his floppy. I wanted it erased cos of the secret Xorandor told us. Well I've told YOU now. We could never check, but we wanted them to go on neutralising warheads, if it WERE true, without anyone knowing. I can't stand broken promises.

And you a politician.

Of sorts. But that's Realpolitik, Pragmatism, Raison d'Etat, many names. Not at all the same thing.

And things have never been the same again between you?

This'll be your room, Tim, my teleport. Used to be Hanjo's room. My son

Ah yes. Very nice. And here's our old friend Poccom 3. I see you've interfaced it with your Intercompatible.

Yes, no problem. But there were two others. The first I may have solved. That secret number. I reread our story and we say that the number Xorandor gave us to reach Xor 7 contained both his own age, four thousand and something years and days, and Xor 7's age, a sort of identity card changing in time, at least that's how we interpreted it. But I'd forgotten that, so naturally my efforts to contact Uther simply on SOFTKEY didn't work, because SOFTKEY contained the Xor 7 number, and for that year I had to look up an old calendar and find out the exact date Xorandor confided Uther and Aurelius to us – he said they'd been born the day before – and replace the Xor 7 numbers with 1 + the years and days since. Luckily the half I memorised was the first half, for of course we never wrote down the number in the narrative and

Jip forgot his half. But I'm almost sure the second half was all those years and days. I hope I've got it right but we can do it again. The second problem's also a case of forgetting. Because I was trying on speculation frequencies in the range between 30 kilohertz and 3 megahertz. But suddenly I remembered that gigahertz episode, and the fact that you'd spent hours getting special waveguides for gigahertz into that reactor – poor Tim, sitting on a bomb, but you were very funny about it afterwards, I can't think how I forgot. And so did Jip. That's why I thought you –
 You were quite right. It's worth a try. And I remembered. I brought the wherewithal.
 Tim, you've a sixth sense.
 No, but I've done a lot of thinking. Of course, we have no idea where these creatures can be, if they are.
 They are, they are, I know it.
 Sure, sure. We'd stand a better chance using a satellite.
 But –
 No satellite is working, I know. But on this frequency, their frequency? And as I say, I brought various electronic adapters and stuff with me. Let me tinker with it for a bit. That coffee has stimulated my fagocites.
 Shaw! Oh, Tim, d'you remember mum?
 Very well. She's done tremendously, hasn't she. I often see her.
 You do?
 On the stage. I've rather lost touch otherwise.
 I'll go down and prepare the lunch. Cold meat and salad I'm afraid, I can't cook in this heat. And iced Moselle, okay? Shout if you need anything.
 No noise. Work on computers is eerily silent. Has he taken it to bits to redo the microcircuits? Or is he trying it on his own? The number's written down in front of him. But he wouldn't know what to type. Oh booles, I'm far too suspicious. And starved, lunch has been waiting for ages and I'm getting drunk on Moselle despite nibbling, and scribbling on the edge of the kitchen table, gazing at the distant hills beyond that awful diplobubble.

Hey, Tim! Lunch is ready.
So am I. And very hungry. All done, Zab.
Oh, Tim, gigavolt! Are you sure?
Can't ever be till we try. I've fixed it on 40 Gigahertz, that's about the highest likely, and we can come slowly down to thirty. We've got all afternoon and evening, anyway. And then tomorrow. But we must eat. This looks great.
I'm half drunk already waiting for you.
Then we'll have to sober you up on more coffee before we start. Gott sei dank for German coffee, I like it better than French or Italian, too bitter. And as for English, it's more like tea with ketchup in it.
Ugh, don't turn my stomach I want to eat.
So you let Jip go without telling him you'd try on your own? Sorry to insist, but I've been trying to contact him and I do have to know what I'm allowed to say.
The answer's yes, I did. I told him I'd thrown away Poccom 3 ages ago, no room. And I had the brainwave about contacting Uther and Aurelius. But he hadn't remembered his half of the number. And suddenly he asked if I'd kept Poccom 3. At least I think so, it's difficult to remember an excited conversation when each item said stimulates another. At any rate, I then suddenly remembered about the Softkey. But presumably he had too and that's why he asked about Poccom 3. I lied. I feel quite ashamed now.
Oh, don't complicate things with guilt.
It would have been a crackerpack opportunity to interface, work on this together and forget what had come between us. I never told him, you see, that I'd discovered he'd kept the story of Xorandor on disc. But I'm sure he knew, he must have tried to look it up and found it erased. I'm sure he was also after that, because he'd forgotten so much of the detail and came to edgetrigger my memory and pick my brainwaves. But the disc would have been even more useful to him. Though even I had to read up about that number. Amazing how one forgets. I found an old diskette you know, by chance, of some quarrel I'd had with our German host in Bayreuth and I'd completely forgotten it, eromed it, not just the content

but the fact there'd been a quarrel.

You mean you'd typed it all into Poccom 3? You screwboole kid.

Afraid so. Very. Even more screwboole to forget.

No, forgetting's the norm, and the best for such episodes.

I screened it for Jip, to sort of make up for being no help, and he too said I was screwboole. Still, I should have cooperated with him. It would have been like the old days.

Yes. And you couldn't do it on your own after all, could you?

Don't kiloword it in! Tim, I've just heard my son's madly in love with a much older woman, an international pilot. She took him to China and as far as I can see left him there. And don't say let him be, I do, I always have. Too much perhaps.

Zab, I said don't blur your state of mind with personal problems, it must be free in case anything happens.

Yes Tim. You're so softalk, so wise, always were, not spiky like me. I was half in love with you at thirteen. Pity I couldn't marry you when I grew up. Coffee's ready.

No sugar. Thanks. I was around thirty at the time, too great a distance, and –

Did you stay with Alex afterwards?

No. We drifted apart. I was offered a job at the B.B.C. pretty soon after the Xorandor affair. Okay, shall we go up?

Yes, I'll carry up the coffee tray. Bring a second chair will you? Oh and the ventilator too, if you can, it gets pretty hot up there in the afternoon, just under the roof.

Wish you'd told me, it was pretty hot by noon.

Yes, sorry, I forgot.

Right, now, you sit in front of Poccom 3 and I'll watch Big Brother here. You must do the typing.

NUMBER.

Zip calling Uther Pendragon. Come in please.

Good, it's come up on the big screen. Wow, lots of interference. Go on. We'll have to be very patient.

Can we just leave it on while we wait? I'm none too keen on broadcasting that number each time, even on Gigahertz that no one uses except for experiments.

No, I'm afraid we have to use it each time if it's like a callsign. We could try and reencode it into SOFTKEY, but that would probably erase the first number for ever.

Who cares? Xor 7's on Mars. No, you're right, better not, you never know, we might need even that! Or Xorandor's number.

Try again.

NUMBER.

Zip calling Uther Pendragon. Come in please.

Blank screen.

Hello Zip. Utha Pendragn calling Zip. How are you?

Tim! It's worked!

Quick! Type something. Anything, Zab but at once. Keep him talking. Try and ask him where he is sometime.

Zip is very pleased to hear from Uther after so many years. Where are you?

Twenty three years three months fourteen days.

So long? You're right! *Where did you go after Zip hid you in the rock hole?*

Beech. By drop. Then up. Onto moving van. Very far.

Uther, where are you now?

Repeat. Very far.

Do you know what is happening to the radio-waves?

Answer yes.

Can you explain why?

Answer no.

Because you don't know?

Answer no.

You can't explain because you don't know or the reason is that you don't know?

Syntax error. The reason for what?

The reason you can't explain is because you don't know or not because you don't know?

The reason is not because I don't know.

Ask him to promise to respond again next time you contact him. Safeguard in case he vanishes.

Uther. Zip wants to remain in contact with you. Will you respond next time I call you up?

I will respond. I respond now.
I asked in case we got cut off.
No cut off.
Are you in touch with Xorandor?
Answer no.
So you never hear from him?
Xorandor is now only a stone on Mars.
Oh no! He's dead!
Cut the emotion Zab, keep the computer-contact.
Did he not get enough radiation?
Answer yes. No food.
Is that why you are eating up our radio-waves?
We are not eating radio-waves. Radio-waves not our food, radiation is our food.
You say "our". Does that mean you are many?
Blank screen.
Are you with Aurelius?
Blank screen.
Uther Pendragon, Zip asks you to come in please.
Blank screen.

9

Random jitters, Tim! It worked! I'd forgotten that rigorous logic, though, one question at a time and all that. But we didn't get much out of him. Takes after Xorandor.

We got quite a bit, some of it negative. First, refusal to give us his position. However, I'd fixed the computer, not only to memorise the frequency we were on but also to estimate the direction. South-East.

Tim, that's maxint. But where?

Can't get the distance without another receiver elsewhere to give a fix, it could be anywhere between here and India. But probably nearer than India. Secondly, refusal to explain the situation, but not because he can't. That's not exactly an admission of responsibility but at least it's one of awareness. And third –

Thirdly he slipped to WE from I, so there's at least more than one. Could just be Aurelius, but he seemed to be generalising about their food, and said OUR FOOD as if he were talking about the whole species.

And it's when you pressed him on that that he shut up.

Yes, absolutely bootloading, and without any kind of sign-off. That never used to happen with Xorandor. Could be a cut but he said there'd be no cut.

Which fourthly looks like another admission of some kind of control over the cuts.

And if so the cut would be another broken promise, I remember how Xorandor insisted on the word promise, but of course that merely meant behaving according to program, and he could never quite accept that humans didn't. And fifthly he said they weren't eating waves.

Well, we know that, Zab. They'd only need to flatten them.

Negentropy. Jip said that. But why?

In other words, he didn't say they weren't altering them, only that they hadn't switched from radioactive particles to radio-waves for food.

But there's food of the mind.

That's an anthropomorphic notion.

No, Tim, it's a metaphor for computer-data. They've always listened to us and recorded everything, and they've been silently storing a constant flow of information about the universe, about the planet and its inhabitants for millions of years. But they never stopped us from hearing the flow until now.

Yes, well, the explanation for that seems clear, once one admits their existence: the sheer quantity is now too much for them. I still don't grasp why it's less effort for them to flatten the modulations so as to reduce all information in the impulses than simply not to record.

Perhaps they can't help recording, they do it automatically and need to do it, the way we breathe. And eat.

Maybe. The problem is still do they exist.

Tim!

Zab, don't be naive. Anyone could have sent those messages.

But –

I mean, anyone working in gigahertz, so that narrows it down considerably, especially now that the waves aren't carriers any more. That would mean one of various teams of technicians all over the place, keeping an ear on things. And out of those, it would have to be someone at least vaguely familiar with the Xorandor story, which did after all hit world headlines twenty years ago, even if it's been forgotten. But many have kept up with it, and not only cranks, some scientists and technicians remained fascinated. It would also have to be someone with a computer, but any such gigahertz technician would automatically have his receiver computer-geared. A sort of very special computer-hack, say.

No, they couldn't fake that peculiar logic. Remember

that only Jip and I discovered how to softalk with Xorandor, the grown-ups depended on Vocal, and Xorandor stopped talking after the hooha, so did his offspring. Nor would these technicians know about Xorandor's information-death from lack of food. Only Jip and I asked him what would happen if he and his offspring didn't get enough radiation on Mars. Another promise not kept.

But anyone could imagine it. The promise was public after all, by all governments concerned. It could even be Jip.

Jip! What do you mean?

You told me he went to Austria on his vacation.

But in the Tyrol! That's not South-East. And he should be in Italy by now. And why should he?

You know your relationship better than I do. You were both such offline kids. He's a much more uptodate expert than I am and he could quite easily have organised a teleport like yours, or gone to some communications centre in Innsbruck or Vienna – the direction was only approximate. Anything is possible in this crazy adventure of yours.

So why did you come, Tim? Why did you go to all that trouble if you're so sceptical?

I'm not only running the B.B.C., Zab, but I'm a scientist, or was, and a scientist must both try every hypothesis and be aware of every possible hoax. A delicate balance. I'm used to the crank-mentality, and the hoax-mentality, not to mention the merely naive, from the floods of letters we receive, there seems to have always been a yearning to rush into print with something merely because one has just thought of it.

Man versteht nicht, was man nicht mit andern teilt.

Translation?

One doesn't understand what one doesn't share with others. It's from one of my favourite authors, nearly half a century ago, Christa Wolf.

I didn't know you went in for literary reading.

It's a marvellous novel, about Kleist. She's very philosophical, that's why I like her. Meanwhile, however, there's absolutely no certainty of ever getting Uther again, though he did say he'd respond. But since he also said there'd be no cut and there was, either from him or from the others, or from whatever Verbivore might be if it's not them, it was more like don't ring me I'll ring you. Oh, what shall I do? We must keep on trying. And so must you. Now that it's all set-up. And now that you'll be more prepared to deal with him, to know what to ask, what to avoid. At night, preferably, when the waves are slightly less crowded.

But Tim, I'm a Euro-M.P.! We're in recess now but even so I'm working on a committee report. And soon I'll have to attend, to receive delegations and so on. It's a full-time job.

Come, let's look at the print-out.

But even rigorous analysis didn't get them much further, Tim told me when he got back. By then, however, and quite suddenly, the whole thing stopped. After a longish spell when even music was interrupted, especially music with words but also other music, so that all our surmises about words were reduced to nothing, suddenly all became normal again. He went to meeting after meeting. All units had reported wholly restored situations from that Saturday afternoon on, no breaks whatever in any transmissions. By Tuesday evening all stations all over the world were repeating all clear, for three whole days, some eighty hours of total media, uncut. The papers were blazing it in huge headlines, though with cautious warnings or perhaps rueful regrets in the smaller print. Government spokesmen, scientists and communications experts were behaving as if they had finally overcome, as expected, a small technical difficulty and were now fully in control again, all the journalists having over-dramatised and fussed too much as usual.

Perry's play A ROUND OF SILENCE was just then due for a repeat, uninterrupted this time, but as the ending was itself a written-in cut many listeners thought Verbivore had begun again, although the announcer's voice came fairly soon to say You have been listening to. They just thought it was temporising.

I have been promoted to Deputy Creative Director, with the usual joke that title entails. Letters to us and to the press mostly tended towards we told you so, expressing anger at the fuss but also relief. Or anti-media and furious. Why is the public always so predictable? When I have these predictable reactions, not all the king's horses would drag me into print with them. I suppose it's all part of the system of knowledge, one has to communicate it. And this at every level, intellectual or foolish. At least for human beings, it doesn't seem to apply to the Xorandor-type creatures.

But Zab will have to learn that as I did, one can't just keep cooped up in a teleport storing and rescreening things. Her life as Euromp seems to be a separated part of her, a role she has forced herself to play to counter her self-sufficiency and strong tendency to withdraw, just as I learnt to play my role at the B.B.C. when I was not allowed to lose myself in Greek and Latin any more. Gradually all our secret treasures have been removed and we've all been made to share the same abstracted and alienating public knowledge. And with deep contradictions. On the one hand for instance, all learning of mere facts, all learning of poetry or multiplication tables by heart had long been condemned and vanished, while on the other hand all television quiz games, with vast prizes at stake, are based on the very type of knowledge that was swept away. Which is why older people often win. Not only did they perhaps get the last vestiges of these structured points of reference, but general knowledge is also something one accumulates painlessly merely by living a long time. Wars in one part of the globe after another over eighty years teach one geography willy nilly, and names of planes and guns and generals. So do catastrophes and scandals and revolutions. And so on. But it irks me that generation after generation of young people is sacrificed for some new theory of teaching methods that insists on jettisoning whatever was good in whatever the previous system was. Like medicine, I suppose, like economic theories, theories of perfect government, theories of peace and war, theories of work and play and leisure and food and wellbeing. So that in the end only those who succeed in finding themselves despite these impositions get by in a reasonable state of health, understanding, and financial independence.

Monday. A whole sixteen days of normal broadcasting!

Some seem to regret it, though most are relieved and have already forgotten the months of Verbivore. The press has dropped the whole topic, the norm never being newsworthy. But then they'd already long got used to the breaks, which had also ceased to be newsworthy, so that when the norm returned it was news, for a few suspenseful days only.

Curious feature, habit. I remember once, long ago, having to drive regularly through a long tunnel, so that my antiquated car radio went silent. I got so used to this that once, when I was driving a colleague, who was talking and talking I was quite surprised when his voice didn't go off the air.

Well, I got into the habit of wordprocessing things long before Verbivore and I'm not going to stop because it has stopped. If it has stopped.

I had the most extraordinary visit this afternoon in my office, from Dawn Trireme, the actress who played Decibel in Perry's play. She'd done it marvellously, her voice getting higher and higher with noise, but lower and lower and fainter whenever threated with silence. Perry's script had it the other way round but we had to correct it, obviously decibels go up with noise. She's rather wasted in radio, she looks so glamorous, and I don't suppose we'll keep her long. She looked radiant, told me she'd been pining away almost to a nervous breakdown during Verbivore, and was so happy it was over. I understood it at first as simple professional anxiety, but to my astonishment and partial fear she seemed to think she WAS Decibel, and DID live on sound. She talked like Decibel, and spoke of Julian, the main character in the play, like an old lover she had as it were possessed. I hardly knew how to handle her, beyond reassuring her she'd always find work in the Drama Department, and telling her of another role I hoped she'd accept. But she really and truly wasn't interested in that aspect at all. Her voice pitched higher and higher as a drill pierced a wall a few offices away, and her eyes looked drugged with ecstasy. Of course, she's a consummate actress and could have put it all on as a joke, but she knows how busy I am and surely wouldn't come and interrupt me just for – no, she really was Decibel, and somehow I felt shaken by the time I managed to get rid of her. I only need a visit from Julian now, who'll be pining away at the RETURN of noise. In fact, I'll call him up, why not. But he has no surname. Or did he? Could look up the script, but no. Julian, what, Julian Ferry, Merry, Derry, that'll do. Jill? Get me Mr Derry will you?

 Julian? Mira Enketei here.
  Mira! I knew it was you. I've been willing you to call me up. Congratulations then. Weak existence, strong will.
 I thought I was dead.
 And I thought you'd be enjoying the silence, recuperating.
 I was, but I could only live to enjoy it by being broadcast again.
 So that revived you? You need noise to exist yet can't stand any other noise but your own voice?
 Mira don't paradox me to perishment.
 Why not, if you live on paradox? We all do, my dear Julian, to a greater or lesser extent, but we're happily not always aware of it.
 And you think making me aware will make me alive? A common delusion of psychoanalysts, who sang Freud with sang-froid for ages. Can I come and see you? I have an idea for a novel.
 No. I'm in radio, not publishing, and far too busy.
 Ah. Because all's normal on the waves again?
 No, I'm always far too busy. We went on as if, you know, we had to keep the airtime constantly filled up, whatever the cuts. We always do, we always did. People can't stand a twenty second silence, they think there's something wrong with their set, and get rattled.
 They had to stand a good deal more than twenty seconds during Verbivore, didn't they?
 Yes. But not any more. All over now.
 All quiet on the wasteful front.
 Hardly. But I'm glad you're okay. I've been vaguely worrying.
 If you'd worried less vaguely I'd have felt more real.
 I had a visit from Decibel an hour ago. She thought she was the actress who played her. If you see what I mean.

Hmm. How is she? Revelling I suppose. By the way, what was the name of the actor who played me? I'd like to contact him.

It's in The Radio Times. We can't give private numbers or addresses but he may be in the book. Or write to him c/o the B.B.C., it'll get forwarded. Bye then, keep well.

This'll get me down if I'm not careful. Seven o'clock, I'd better go home. Or no, everyone's gone, I'll lock the door and wordprocess, that'll get me straightened out.

Nothing. Blank screen, as Zab's experience would say. Well, I'm glad all's returned to normal. Or am I? It was rather exciting, especially her contacting Uther. Surely it can't just end there? Maybe I'm hungry, I think I'll go to the canteen.

Sunday, 2100. It's happened. The return of Verbivore, and with a vengeance. At 1500 hours yesterday. Exactly three weeks after Zab's contact, if that means anything. However, it's not just breaks now but total silence, on every type of frequency, on every type of material. I had exactly the same reactions as the first time, I assumed that my radio was phut. I tried the TV and assumed the same. But then I quickconnected – if that's the right word for such a slow reaction. Tried to ring Tim but the phone was dead too. I still half-assumed it was only me. Funny that, apparently everyone else reacted in much the same way, according to the Sundays, who've had a field-day. Still cautious though, the new shut-down was only a few hours old when they went to press. But they all report total blackout since three Saturday. They can't contact their correspondents anywhere so they're assuming it's worldwide. The airport journalists had to rush in by taxi (subway halted because no kind of intercom), to say that all planes are grounded and none were landing, and all those landing at the time of the cut-off had a dangerous time of it, one crashed, no survivors. No intercomputer links working.

They make it all sound very dramatic indeed. No one had imagined quite that during the time that Verbivore was only partial and intermittent, though various scare-scenarios were written up. You'd have thought they would have organised contingency plans, but no, everyone made do with occasional cuts. Most of the pages in the Sundays are prepared well in advance, so they're still fat, but they had to redo the main news pages and some have brought out these scare-scenarios. I suppose we'll get nothing but those now, since they're bereft of news, so they'll fill their space with speculations, with verbal reports from local journalists who've managed to reach their offices as well as members of the public who'll be hammering to be allowed in and tell their tale or get explanations and reassurances.

It's amazing that the papers could be distributed at all. By van here in London, yes, but are the intercity and suburban trains working? I assume trains need intercom just like the subway. There's going to be a rush on buses and cars and petrol and a total clogging of the road network. And paralysis of every activity that depends on radio-communication, on the telephone and on computer-networks. All activities that need constant information, in other words travel, trade, medicine, education, sport, games, politics, research, wars, defence watchfulness, diplomacy, the lot: war and peace.

We'll have to depend on personal contact. And on our imaginations.

10

Dear Sir,

As usual the experts have misled us, saying what governments wanted them to say. It took fifty or more years for nuclear scientists to admit that nuclear tests and stations could be dangerous, fifty or more years for cigarette-makers to stop their reassuring parallel research, fifty or more years for industrial chemists to admit that certain products destroy the ozone layer or the natural environment, fifty or more years for economists to admit that 1929 type crashes are after all possible even if "different" or that pure profit creates misery, as many for doctors to admit that strong medical drugs are eventually self-defeating, need I go on? At every election candidates talk about having only the good of the people at heart. No wonder the electorate is disaffected and self-disenfranchised, so that a 51% majority for anyone now represents only something like 21% of any constituency. Perhaps we should offer prizes to electors who bother to vote, as in the entertainment industry.

Yours, etc.

> M.K. Richards, President,
> Society for the Protection
> of People from Their Rulers.

Dear Sir,

I can't reach my son in Burma and can't even get pictures of the troubles there because of Verbivore and I am disgusted at your jubilation. It does wonders for your circulation figures no doubt but is nothing sacred?

Yours,

> Mary Kimberley,
> Wimbledon.

Editor: Far from being jubilant, we are as distressed as you are. We can't get the news to you either.

Dear Sir or Madam,
Why didn't governments prepare contingency plans for this contingency? They had plenty of warning practice didn't they?
Yours sincerely,
      A Student.

Dear Sir,
We miss the TV games that kept the family together. It was hard enough to keep the kids off the street and away from the drug-pushers. Now there's only the pictures and they cost money we can't send them every night. Your games pages are a rotten substitute and games boxes in shops cost money too and aren't the same without the host. Why don't they set up halls everywhere to run the TV games in every district and every village after all the TV games had live audiences.
Yours faithfully,
      Emma Talbot,
      Tottenham.

Dear Sir,
Hurray, people will have to learn self-reliance again.
Yours,
      T. Cuthbert,
      Liverpool.

Dear Sir,
Will someone please explain to us poor nitwits what is happening in simple terms we can understand? Your reports are far too technical, we're not all radio-hams or electronic engineers.
Yours sincerely,
      J. Pemberton,
      North Riding.

Dear Sir,
How are we to achieve national visibility without the media? May I remind you that national visibility is an exponent of media-effect, both integral and fractional, both negative and positive. We also risk the erosion of institutions dependent on performative utterance.
Yours,
      W.L. Norbert,
      Gloucester School of
      Communications Studies.

Dear Sir,
   Twenty years ago I was a "witness" (of a kind) of the Xorandor affair in Carn Tregean, Cornwall. I was the local policeman and I even lost an eye in one of the demos. I had to eventually accept anticipated retirement and I need TV. But even at that time we were insufficiently informed. The cult activities down here continue, although "Xorandor" has long been removed. But I distinctly recollect that there were offspring, and that the "creatures" had unusual communicative powers. All were expedited to Mars on account of the threat to the nuclear deterrent which they represented. That was another "theory" we were told to live by, but which was abandoned when the Soviet Union supposedly changed heart with Glazz-nots.
   What I desire to know is this: Were they really expedited? Could any of the "creatures" have survived and reproduced? Could they be at the source of all our troubles?
   Yours sincerely,
                    Bill Gurnick,
                    Carn Tregean, Cornwall.

Dear old Bill! I knew him well alas poor Yorick. Aren't these letters hilarious, Jip? So, you're stuck in London. Everyone's stuck everywhere. Lucky I'm resting or I might have been stuck in Melbourne or anywhere. How did you get this far? And why isn't your family with you?

I'd sent them home a week before, must have had a hunch. In fact no, the kids had to go to camp. I managed to rent a car in Austria. The ferries are still running somehow, on eye-navigation, okay in August but it'll soon be dangerous. They don't run in morning mist or after dark, it's affecting all radar too, you know. I waited three days to get on.

But why didn't you stay in Austria? Much nicer to be stuck there.

No. I have colleagues to see here. Among which Tim, at the B.B.C. He wrote to me at Nasa, weeks ago, I only got the letter in Austria because it was marked urgent. That's what decided me.

But why, pet? You haven't seen him for years.

He had an idea about the alphgaguys being responsible, and something we might do together. I'd had the same idea myself, and tried to discuss it with Zab, but she was most uncooperative.

Ah yes, Isabel. She's changed, you know.

We all do, mum.

And Tim! So pompous. He came to see me the other day and kept trying to impress me with his connections. The Prime Minister, you know, invited me to Chequers, he said, and he's the only person the P.M. listens to on this, according to him. Wanted to understand all the technicalities and listened most avidly. No, Prime Minister, you can't do that, he told me he'd say, and Sir Timothy, this, Sir Timothy that, he'd quote the replies, this just to remind me all the time that he's been knighted, only recently anyway, as if that could impress a senior Dame like me. Besides, one doesn't quote people saying one's title in reported conversation, it's not done.

That sounds most unlike Tim.

You'd be surprised.

Why did he come and see you?

Well, I invited him, actually, for a drink. I'd written to the Director-General about, well, a professional matter, and got a rather curt letter from Tim instead, so after a few months I wrote him a little personal note to tick him off and make peace at the same time.

Did you learn anything?

About what, dear?

About Verbivore, mum, Logfag, whatever you prefer to call it.

Oh, that. No, of course not, beyond the usual banalities about public deprivation. He'd consider me too brainless to understand the technical aspect, which even I am beginning to grasp after your explanations, the political aspect, the social and psychological aspects, the legal aspect, it's all become such a bore. Apart from not being able to use the telephone, which is rather a nuisance, and the rush on secondhand bookshops, I don't miss the media at all, after all, everyone got on very well without them in earlier times. On the contrary, it's sending people en masse to the theatre again. Did I tell you I've been asked to play Lady Bracknell at the National? A HANDbag?

How do I do it? Thank you. Well, he had the good manners just to be affable. He did apologise for his letter though, said it was written by one of his assistants and he'd merely signed it without looking. Much overworked, poor dear, with all this crisis. He didn't stay long. When are you seeing him?
 In about half an hour. Must go. I'll get a taxi.
 You'll be lucky.
 If he's so busy he'd probably keep me waiting even if I arrived on time. See you later mum. I'll be in this evening.

I was late of course, can't get used to this paralysis. The tubes and commuter trains are running but much more sparsely and slowly. So there are immense queues for buses and taxis and a clog of private cars, though the British are all being very war-effortish and giving lifts.

Tim was very pleased to see me and not at all pompous, no name-dropping or title-wearing, mum must have invented that, or pinched it from some play. He was very business-like and technical. We exchanged telecom news and theories in a comforting scientific way. Comforting because it was real nice to see him again as an equal after all these years. He's thoroughly up to the minute with all we're doing so we didn't spend long on electromagnetic chitchat and rival theories. Nor on the wonderful way the British are responding, developing messenger services and so forth – but there's nothing particularly Brit about that, I guess we're way ahead there, all the more so for the distances we have to cover. He came straight to the point. Or rather, I thought at first it wasn't the point and he just wanted to chat me up. He asked me if I'd seen Zab on my way back from Austria.
 No. I'd seen her in June.
 But surely you had to drive up the motorway via Aachen?
 I came by HST from Milan. Very slow in fact, but cars are too dangerous now that the telecomp system isn't working and everyone's driving manically as they used to twenty years ago.
 That's a very elaborate explanation, could you be feeling guilty?
 Garbage, Tim. I just had my mind on other things. As it was

I waited three days in Zeebrugge to get on a ferry. No chances at all at Ostend or Calais and the tunnel's blocked too, working but trains rare and slow. And all because of no intercom. They're all being buffering over-cautious. But you probably disagree.
  Yes, Jip. You should have seen Zab, though. She had news for you.
  News? What sort of news? How do you know? You mean –
  She rang me urgently about six weeks ago and I went over. We made contact with Uther Pendragon.
  What!
  Ah. So it wasn't you?
  Me? What d'you mean, me?
  There was just a faint possibility. A joke, you know. Endjoke. But how did –
  On Poccom 3. She'd linked it up to her Intercompatible. And I set it up on Gigahertz. She'd worked out the secret number for Uther, the other one having contained the ages of both Xorandor and Xor 7.
  Why, the itsybitsy –
  Debug, Jip. She was very sorry she'd lied to you. She told me why, and you know why, so don't let's go into that. She said she'd let pass a great chance for you two really to get together again.
  So she kept Poccom 3!
  Yes. She'd been trying on it for ages without luck, so she called me. She'd forgotten the Berkeley 2 communication lark was on Gigahertz. So I tinkered with her whole set-up – just like the hooha, remember? Except that she has a much more advanced computer. No problem, and I hooked it to the B.B.C. Satellite. She said I could tell you. Here's the print-out. Copy, you may keep it.
  I read the print-out [attached]. I admit I was non-plussed, as Xorandor used to say.
  Jumping nukes! (as I used to say). Though it could be a hoax. Any computer-hack technician on duty –
  Yes, and I warned her. But she insisted that only you and she knew certain things, the syntax traps, for instance, and

the possibility of Xorandor's circuit-death. Information-death, she called it.

True. Though easily enough imaginable by anyone who'd followed or looked up the public Xorandor story.

I said that too. What do you think?

Did you go on trying?

Yes, all weekend, without luck. It was the Saturday when everything suddenly returned to normal, almost immediately after, as it later turned out, the moment when he cut himself off, or got cut off. He said "no cut-off", yet was cut-off, and Verbivore stopped. Could be coincidence, but it did seem as if he had some sort of control, if not at that moment, then at least immediately afterwards.

And yet the norm only lasted three weeks. It's as if all that had happened before had only been warnings.

Or rehearsals. Testing their technical capacities in each domain before the real thing. They'd even had a go at music, music with words at first, then all music.

Have you any idea whether Zab –

Has gone on trying? Yes. In vain so far. She writes me brief sitreps every two days. Late of course. Brief because there's nothing to report. And then she's back in session now and can't spend much time at it. I think you should try and go back to Aix, Jip.

What? After what –

I told you, she's very sorry. And you cheated first, Jip.

But I was only a kid. Why hold it against me all these years? Besides, she was wrong, I was right. If we had the original text today we might get inklings from it, things we've forgotten.

She does have it. She copied it before erasing yours.

Jumping –

Nukes, yes.

It had crossed my mind, but I never thought – I mean I thought it was on sheer principle she erased it, and maybe to punish me for not keeping my promise, but I gave her the benefit of the doubt on the principle. Whereas in fact –

It was pure revenge? Pure spite? Nothing is ever pure, Jip.

You could also say she's now realised you were right. At any rate, she does have it. That's all that matters now.

Well, let her get on with the job, then, I have to get back to mine.

You're stuck here, Jip, Nasa knows that.

Nonsense, they wrote to me at my mother's address to say they'd booked me on one of the old steamers. There's a queue of course, but they have influence.

When?

End of September.

Plenty of time for Aix, then. Be forgiving, Jip. The crisis is more important than your mutual resentments. She saw that.

But why should I be able to help? More than you could I mean. You noticed she used Zip, the call-sign for Jip and Zab. Don't tell me Uther, if it was him, can read behind call-signs and knew there was only one of us and must have both! That voice-recognition business on mike was a purely local and temporary development of Xorandor's, passed on to his offspring, true, but obviously unused all this time. Oh I know he had sophisticated sensing and emitting devices, electric to pressure transducers or something, but his vocal capacity was a gadget, which he developed only to contact us – oh stubs, here I am attributing a purpose, I'm as bad as Zab,

It's not their voice that might be in question here, it's yours and Zab's. So far, however it's only screen connection, and may remain so even if we do recontact, you're right, no voice comes into it.

That's what I'm saying. Anyone could intercept and come in, this isn't Berkeley 2 and the supervan. I still don't see what I could do.

You're much more scientifically competent now than she is, or indeed than I am after years of admin. You might think of a way. And you lived it all, and could now read it up, you'd be much more helpful than me if anything did occur. She'd accept that. After all she didn't hesitate to appeal to me.

Why didn't she appeal to me then? I was only in Austria, she had my address and number.

Don't demand too much, Jip. First steps are difficult. Hence me.

The go-between.

If you like. But it's worth a try.

I don't see what anyone can do now, however competent, if no contact of any kind is possible on radio-waves.

We keep quite a few of our receivers permanently open, just in case. Zab must be doing the same. I don't know, Jip, you might think of something. Perhaps with the air so empty some very special messages from you might be possible, and be received. After all, plenty of people are trying, on the same principle. In any case this occurred on thirty-eight gigahertz, hardly a crowded channel even when the air isn't empty. Please go to your hotel and think about it, and if you go, leave me a note at the desk downstairs, or just post it.

I'm not at a hotel I'm at mum's. I have thought about it. Can you use your influence to get me on a ferry, or even the tunnel-train?

I'm not sure, I'll try. Everyone's trying, though, and without phones it's – Here, I'll write you a letter, you can take it with you.

So that's the conv as I recorded it, no time for trimmings. As for the technical conv, I learnt nothing I didn't know so I quietly effaced it when the talk about Zab started. A drama-producer called Mira Inkytie or something came in just as I left to say one of her authors was stuck in Moscow. But how does she know if there's no communication anywhere in the world?

11

The Soviet Wordprocessors' Union liked A ROUND OF SILENCE, they couldn't believe it was broadcast before Verbivore (or Slovoyed as it's called here) and that I'd actually written in a radio-cut. Vestiges of sociorealism I suppose, can't imagine what doesn't happen, and of course technical hitches couldn't be admitted even if they occurred. I had to produce the script, with the date, to convince them. My talk was a great success.

In fact things are still rather drab here despite Postsocialism and the stained-glaznost opening on the West. Many more goods available in the shops since my last visit fifteen years ago, and a more relaxed atmosphere. But people still can't get out of the country easily, except for unwanted troublemakers, and since they never believed their media anyway they don't seem to miss them. Not that this is admitted by anyone in the Wordprocessors' Union, they're all state-supported and state-promoted still. I'm trying to meet some non-members, not exactly dissidents, who aren't recognised, but ordinary processors whose existence is on the contrary proudly proclaimed now, like a puppet opposition or a tolerated Society of Permanent Protestors. Accused at most of lateral thinking. Those free not to belong, they say. I imagine that means they have to earn their living some other way. As most of us do in the West, not alas by teaching any more, at least not literature, but by processing for TV if we can, the last big buyer of fiction. I'm always being promised some meeting or other, but nothing happens, or else it's cancelled at the last minute. It's as if I were being screened from all but the official wordprocessors. And unfortunately I depend on these for contacts. He's away in his dacha, they say, or she's on holiday in the Crimea, and he lives in Gorbachevgrad. Anyway they say it's too far, such a big country you know, especially now that all planes are grounded.

I would have liked to know if any one misses foreign broadcasts, or if that too is a myth, a B.B.C. myth, a Voice of America myth, from the ancient jamming days.

I'm stuck here anyway. Or rather, if I'm to go back to the West by slow non-teleguided train I'd rather explore Russia that way. This is being organised by Juri Piatigorski but it's taking time, the trains are overcrowded and very few. Everyone always was on the move here, seeing their families at the other end of the Union, but the last forty years had seen much improvement in internal air traffic. And now it's all back to the mid-twentieth century again. Yuri says I should go North to Gorbachevgrad while it's still warm (but no mention of an introduction to the processors I want to meet there, I'm evidently to go as mere tourist) then down through the Ukraine towards Crimea as the winter comes.

But shall I have enough money? Money! he says, you Westerners are all the same. I meant of course paper-money, now that magnetic cards don't work, and they have been cumbersomely slow in printing it. At the moment they're simply handing me the new ruble notes in small quantities, promising travellers' cheques, whatever those are, and if they're like our old cheque system I don't see what use they can be if the banks have no notes to hand out. But he didn't seem to understand. Do not anguish yourself, your Perry Stroyka books have been selling like hot cookies and will ably cover the voyage and even comfortable hotels, yes, we have those too, even in little towns, however says your old-dated propaganda, this is POST-socialism. But I cannot wager for the trains since Slovoyed. We have not first class you know.

Of course not. Their top officials went by car or plane, and when they couldn't for some reason they had those special sealed luxury carriages I've heard about, that no one can see into, though they can see out. Presumably they've made a few special trains with only those, not listed. All part of the protocollage.

Well, they're certainly generous, they've lent me an American PC I can type on so I'm keeping a traveller's journal of sorts. Thank Verbivore internal computing isn't affected or I'd go flipflop with frustration. But journals are so "old-dated" as Yuri calls it we've all forgotten how to keep them so it's just a chatterscreen. Nor am I any good at travelogue. I mean Moscow's sublime, the centre anyway, but I'm much more interested in atmosphere and people, and the atmosphere and therefore the people or vice versa are very peculiar. Russians have always been cut off so they're used to it, but they're a very warm-hearted lot when you do meet them, and when they're not frightened – which they still are at odd, very odd moments, if one says something out of place or if they see someone they somehow depend on.

So in a way they go on as before, visiting each other and talking in the street. But the telephone silence is getting them down. For decades they never used it as much as we did because it was so inefficient, Juri says. (And of course insecure). But in the last ten years a huge effort was made towards a super microwave-network that reaches every tiny village of the outmost steppes, and which did more to keep the population happy than any sudden flood of consumer goods or shower of exit visas. They were very proud of it, and it was cheap too. Mothers and fathers and sons and daughters and lovers and cousins and friends were in constant touch. Then it became more touch and go. And now nothing, total deprivation.

The other peculiar aspect is the combination of complete political scepticism with an avid hunger for news, news of any kind. They pore over the newspapers and queue to read the sheets posted on the special placards, as in the old days. I suppose that generations of censorship and officialese have taught them, with their mother's milk, to read between the lines, to hear between the sentences, to see behind the images. And that skill, that special secret pleasure, is now taken away from them, except for the newspapers. The same of course is happening in the West and indeed all over, but there was much less reading beyond the said, since all was over-explicit, and what reading-beyond there was would be less for political manoeuvring than for scandal. Anatol, a friend of Yuri's, told me that terrorists would disappear in the West now that the media can't give them publicity. Here they were never given publicity so they didn't operate – except abroad by remote control of course. So the withdrawal symptoms for the unsaid concern other types of fantasy behind the dead lines and inside the head. You would think that after ninety years or more of this a strange wild poetry would emerge, but as far as I can judge from translations and hearsay it hasn't. Though maybe hearsay is strictly controlled too.

Tuesday. Still here, a whole week later. Too troubled to write it up – mostly sight-seeing and receptions – for yesterday I met a sublime creature at a party given for me by Yuri. She's called Natalia Narodovna and writes poetry on a dual-program computer. I don't understand how it works but she told me she can mix lines and cut-in stanzas, or paras, or whatever she said she composes in, and mix languages too. Sounds a bit as if she's just discovered Surrealism, or Burroughs, or Jandl – the lot probably, forbidden before, but anyway she's ravishing. Oh no, no politics, she said, except as a cut-in, you know, for IRONY. Seems she'd just discovered that too. Her ochy weren't churnia but deep violet blue and her hair was bright green and spiked out in an eighties Western style, I forget what they called it. Most fetching. Her breasts weren't in any style or ism, just lusciously eye-dragging and finger-tempting. And her buttocks! I asked her to come with me on my long journey and teach me Russian, but she just stared at me, was it dreamily, hungrily, angrily, shyly, prudely, calculatingly, indifferently? I couldn't translate that stare. Then someone took her away.

But this morning at eight – I wasn't even up or shaved – she called on me at the hotel. They couldn't ring my room so she just came up. She walked in, wearing a yellow cotton dress below her green hair and violet eyes, and carrying a silverfox fur-coat. She laid this over a chair and sat on the bed.

Said she'd left her luggage downstairs but it would be brought up. We'd be leaving at six tomorrow morning. She had to go out to buy a few more things for the winter, which starts early here, but she'd be back for lunch. I had better buy some things too, she said, she could help me in the afternoon, and she started opening the wardrobe and drawers to see what I had. She took out a notebook and jotted down items I lacked, muttering in Russian. Then she came back to the bed, kissed me lightly on the forehead, showing me her breasts as she leant, and was off.

Am I imagining all this? Was I awake or did I dream it? Hard-on proof of neither.

Will she bring her dual-program computer with her and will it come between us?

Is she a beautiful-spy-trap? Will she come to the hotel with me after the shopping, for dinner, and then, to this room? And oh! Is that a two-way mirror, like the dual-program computer, with a very special effects camera behind?

I am imagining it all. We're several decades safely past 1984 now and peace has long been declared between the two blocks, at least at the surface. Was Gorbachev really a Potemkin, and caught us all in his bag of media-activities and diplotricks, so that all is back as it was forty years ago, but under a serene surface? Or was he brought down by the old guard so that all is back as it was forty years ago under a serene surface? Either way, I must beware. Or am I still a prisoner of old Western myths, as Yuri calls them? The trouble is, it wouldn't even make good copy for a novel, it's all so old fur-hat. And no one knows I'm here, except the Embassy, and they won't care two chips, or if they do they won't be able to do anything but bootload.

I must have dreamt it all, it's so banal. Poor analysts, how bored they must get. At least we writers process our own garbage. What spikes me is the feeling that I caused it all, by imagining Verbivore before it happened – of a sort, I never imagined this much. Or maybe it's all Mira's fault. Probably she imagined the whole thing and it occurred and got out of hand. Sorcerer's apprentice inside her damn whale. But then everyone's like that, politicians, economists, scientists, the lot. Until now only they could put their fantasies into effect, whereas we never had that power and remained harmless babblers, meticulously agencing our monsters in stepwise refinement and descrambling them at will, or else time did that for us, dumping them into erased memories. Perry Hupsos indeed! The subliminal sublime. Perry Striker in derring-deed. Mira Enketei I hate you. Natalia Narodovna I love you.

We're all in technical unemployment, save for a skeleton staff just in case it all stops, or rather starts again, depending on what I mean by "it". Many of us have been temporarily transferred to data-analysis, past data that is, since no more data of occurrences are available, except those of public reaction and sociological fallout, as they call the resulting behaviour. I'm on socio-fallout, which seems predictable, except that no-one really bothered to imagine it when they could, and there are as always some unexpected side-effects.

We're of course severely handicapped in our data-gathering by the telephone silence, and physical displacement is restricted to those whose business is strictly necessary to economic survival, theirs and the nation's, in other words those who can still go to and from work. But technical unemployment is rising by the minute, in most firms and factories, shops and offices that depended on international or even intercity computer networks, they're paralysed, and only the few lame ducks that escaped the innumerable lean-and-fit programs of the past can now function, and are not only flourishing but overwhelmed with demand: handicrafts, tailors and dressmakers, manual work such as building and repairs, d.i.y shops, small repair garages, food shops that fetch and carry their own supplies, offices that kept typewriters or can manage on internal computer functions, politicians, lawyers, street-cleaners and the like – the last three categories having never ever been out of work since they all have to deal with human dirt. People can actually feel and see what they buy again, instead of receiving plastic-wrapped packages of objects bought via teleshopping, with screws that don't fit, or cartons of domestic appliances with a carefully unstamped guarantee inside.

But most people are temporarily suspended on half-pay, which they have to collect themselves at unemployment centres, and these soon run out of the new paper money that has had to be rushed into print, and have to send constant groups of armed messengers to the banks. Gone are the days of payment by plastic card and computerised transfers.

At home, people have nothing to do, no telly, except videocassettes, no radio, only discs, no shopping or playing games or partner-hunting by minitel – the titillophone as it's called. The young are out on the streets, inventing their own games, chiefly gang warfare, drugs and mugging, now that handbags contain money again, and rape.

On the other hand, international terrorism has vanished from the scene as if by magic. No more planes to hijack of course, but even ship- or train-hijack, and carbombs, and bus or building explosions have stopped. No point, if there are no cameras and journalists to come upon the scene afterwards and give lots of publicity. No point, if the news isn't broadcast immediately and a claim of responsibility on behalf of this or that group can't be phoned in twenty-four hours later. This, however, may be a total illusion on the part of those who have always and long believed that they make the news, that without them there would be no news. Maybe local violence is continuing everywhere, just as it is on the streets, and local wars, everywhere, ancient tribal wars between Persians and Arabs, Jews and Palestinians, blacks and whites, Hindus and Moslems, Tamils and Singalese, Hongkongians and Chinese, Koreans and Koreans, Arabs and Arabs, Utus and Tutsis, peoples and presidents. Only we don't hear about them any more. As for the many hostages that have been languishing in secret jails all over the place for years, that technique of pressure thrived on secrecy, as in the Crusades, and never depended on radio-communication or even the media, who only intermittently remembered to mention them and fuss slightly. International finance is paralysed.

The English are being suddenly cooperative again, visiting each other in their homes, bringing their music, their games, food and comfort for the old. Or, as the Prime Minister said (in the papers), British public life will continue to go on. But many are peculiarly helpless, staying indoors and moping or agonising from media withdrawal symptoms. Many write to the press, long illiterate letters, only a tiny percentage of which, I'm told, can be published, despite the game efforts of editors to run papers run by the people. YOU are now the news, they print, write to us how you feel, what you're doing, how you're coping, share with others the bright ideas you have for the weathering of this difficult period. For period it is, dear readers, like a national war, a world war even, and everyone must do his bit for the war effort, shoulder to the wheel...

The cinemas are packed, and the theatres, and the music-halls, the concert-halls, the art-galleries, the museums, the old libraries, the disco-, the cine-, the videotheques, the sports stadiums, but not for Fling and Broody or Rock concerts, singers being lost without a mike. Queues start hours beforehand and street-artists entertain them and pass the hat round as in the nineteenth century, not for coins, those disappeared years ago, but for small paper money. All the old films scheduled for television have been pounced on by the film companies and old halls reopened as extra cinemas. Video-shops are cleaned out, and there's been a similar rush on audio-cassettes for walkmans. Diskette bookshops are doing fine, and the few second-hand book shops are now emptied and closed down. Bingo-halls and pinball alleys, indoor sports, outdoor sports, everyone is jogging, marathoning, cross-countrying, cycling, tennising, riding, horse-drawn caravaning. Motorbikes, cars, vans and trucks are severely restricted to essential communications and supplies since the obligatory telecomputer-guidance system collapsed, and besides, petrol is in very short supply because tankers can only navigate by vision and North Sea oil ran out long ago. No radar works and all war-readiness is meaningless. Some people are insisting in the press that maverick planes are bound to have a go at illegal transport, now that all the aircraft in the world are grounded. Foolish to publish the idea, but I suppose someone would have thought of it and has thought of it already, only we don't know. And some are naturally going further and saying that any (supposedly abolished) nuclear missile could be launched and guided upon us wholly undetected, thus neutralising all (supposedly abolished) deterrent reaction.

Perhaps the eeriest result, however, is not these imagined threats, but the actual existence of cosmonauts up there in the Indo-American and Franco-Russian space-stations, circling on their orbits, totally incommunicado. Presumably the stations can function on their internal computers and hitec, but we can't know whether they are functioning or not. We can't even know whether they're alive, and how long they can hold out – in principle years, but how long will Verbivore continue?

As for governments and administrations, they're practically at a standstill. All the vast enterprise of modernisation that had occurred, long after everyone else had been submitted to it, at the end of the last century, is suddenly as useless there as in industry, and civil servants, presumably everywhere, have had to go back to endless papers and penpushing. And naturally they aren't numerous enough to cope. Here some provisional recruitment is being made, but few have the training and experience required. I suspect, however, that after the first dismay politicians and civil servants are now secretly relishing the disappearance of media-hounding, which they enjoyed from vanity but cursed from an atavistic preference for acting without informing. As for the police, it is also incapacitated by the loss of quick communication. Back to the whistle and the bobbies on the beat. The Navy, what's left of it and including surfaced nuclear submarines, is reduced to local eye-navigation, the Army to old-fashioned exercises on Salisbury Plain, the Air Force is grounded. Crime flourishes. Crime never did get computerised, except for computer-crime.

So all in all the best and worst of the British – and I suppose it's so in all other countries – has come out into full expression during these peculiar times of Verbivore. People are in fact actually speaking to each other again. What has vanished is the non-local, the national, the international opening out on and speaking to each other. If, that is, mankind ever was on speaking terms.

12

The lady in my office is stunningly beautiful, but I can't make out what she wants. She whispers or murmurs inaudibly as if personally affected by Verbivore. She talks English and isn't even from my constituency, though I have people waiting outside. She was introduced as Miss Dawn Trireme, but keeps calling herself Decibel, and me Isabel, although I've never met her. Says it makes a nice sound, and repeats softly, Isabel – Decibel, Decibel – Isabel.

What exactly are you representing, or requiring, Miss – er –

Decibel, I'm, dying, please, help, me.

But I'm not a doctor, I'm a politician.

Silence. Which seems to say, same thing.

Do you want me to call a doctor? Do you know what you think you're dying of?

Of, radio, si, lence.

Everyone's pretty sick with that.

You don't, under, stand. I, mea, sure, sound.

Oh I see. (*A nut*). Well, there's still plenty of other noise around. Even in this office.

There, are, lots, of, me, around. But I'm a, special, Deci, bel. I, live, on, radio, sound, in houses, in po, lice cars, in navi, gation, units, every, where.

This speech visibly exhausts her, she looks demolished.

Oh. (*Humouring her*). Why? Too refined? Surely you can measure all noise.

No. Dis, tri, bu, tion, of, labour. Some, of, us, have, spe, cial, assign, ments.

That seems an antiquated system these days of polyvalence and flexibility.

Please, Isa, bel, don't, waste, pre, cious, time, on, comment, ary. It's, the, res, ponsa, bility, of the, Creator, he's, always, crea, ting, a pre, ce, dent, and, ma, king, a scene. We can't, change, the, basics. But you, could, alter, some, para, meters, you, could, get, radio, and TV, on the, air, again. I, need, it, desper –

Me? But how?

Silence.

How do you know I'm involved, competent?

Silence.

I'll see what I can do, I added, the way I answer my electors.

Still no answer. She died, there in her chair.

Dialogue in dreams usually gets garbled, fluffed, one knows the exact content but can't hear the actual words, or at least one can't reproduce them even immediately after, except by reconstruct. But here the words were as clear as if I'd recorded them, they still rang (or rather murmured) in my memory-ear. They were even visually clear, as if I'd already typed and screened them, or like the dialogue windows of a computer.

I saw the other complainers till seven, all Germans from Aachen Kreis as they should be, in a sort of haze, promising to look into all their woes. And when I got home, I found Jip on the doorstep. Everyone arrives on the doorstep these days since they can't ring, and each time I wonder who it will be. But I was surprised. Or rather no, only half-surprised since I'd been half-expecting him. Curious, how women have to sow the seed in men's minds and then wait patiently till it sprouts as their own idea. No, that's not fair, I did lie to him. But I didn't expect him to believe me.

He said he'd talked to Tim (that too, I'd expected, though Tim never mentioned it, but then he's too busy to write). He was very affectionate, and I was glad and responded generously. Our bygones don't have to be verbally let be, they just are. He offered his help. Two softwares better than one. AND voice perhaps, maybe, who knows, maybe they still function on that. But he wanted to screen the old Xorandor floppy and trigger-edge his memory. Had I reread it? Yes of course, found those important details about gigahertz and the access number. He might find other things. He wanted to start talking at once.

Not tonight, Jip, I'm too tired.

Oh. Okay. Yes, your face does look rather like a satellite weather map.

Clouds jerking southwestwards from the right eye to the left corner of the mouth? Thank you.

But I said it laughing, and showed him to his room. That is, to the teleport. And gave him access to everything. Even the number, to show absolute trust reestablished. I suggested he read Xorandor tonight after dinner and we'd try tomorrow, together. Meanwhile, come down and have a drink and help me get something to eat.

The meal was pleasant, all tension gone, no recriminations on either side. Seems we've really recovered our old twin-relationship, hope it lasts, we've each become so spiky. He only made one reference to my isolation, my leaning ivory tower he called it, but it was friendly and not aggressive. In fact, the whole thing was effortless, if not exactly telepathic yet. Too cool and dark for the terrace now but we faced the suburban lights and the Big Bubble Gum, sparkling from within, at the small table in the living-room.

He's stuck in Europe. Everyone's stuck. Hanjo's stuck in China. I had one other letter from him. Says he's located his father, at a huge technical (tecnical) centre in Manchuria, no details, and is making his way there. His teacher friend helped him apparently through the burocracy (beaurocracy). Clever boy! I wondered if it was the Kirin Polytechnic he'd studied at, or really "new"? And what technology? So I asked the head of a Chinese delegation what centre, and he was rather suspicious at first and said Manchuria was as large as Europe, but when I explained that I was only trying to locate my son, who was with his father (that's anticipating a bit), and said it was a "huge NEW" technical centre, he replied that it could be the Communications Centre at Harbin. He pronounced it Hairpin, but I found it on the map. Jip was sympathetic but only triggered up his interest when I mentioned this last item. Apparently one of the concentrations of occurrence (when there was activity to cut) had been mapped in Manchuria, he thought in Heilungkiang way up North but he could be misremembering. Perhaps you could go on another data-determining trip, he said.

And live happily ever after? Not so easy to organise, Jip.
The living happily or the trip?
Both. No time for a slow boat to China. And I've already been. And I am happy.

He hadn't come straight here, he told me, but first gone to Paris, to look up old Lagache, remember him? At that first meeting in Harwell, transmitted by one of Xorandor's offspring? He'd met up with him at a conference a few years ago and they'd exchanged addresses. Lagache was one of those who'd continued to work on the alphaguys, on and off. He had to go to Vienna this week and promised to take a microwave expert with him to try and get a second bearing on the same frequency.

Wow! But what if it isn't the same?

Don't worry, the air's so empty of signals he'll find. I also saw Andrewski in England. He's at UKAEA now, counter-braindrain.

Pale podgy Slav.

No, Zab. I remember how nonplussed you were when he appeared on German TV, and he was dark with narrow eyes, contrary to your insane commentaries. Strange you should remember your invented description and not the real man.

Dark tartar type, yes! So you do remember details! The irrelevant ones, you used to say. Yet they stuck!

Nonsense, I've seen the man recently. I have the memory of an elephant cracking a nut in a china-shop.

Or a chip in a microcomputer. It's a hammer. And a bull.

What's a bull?

I wonder if feminists are calling female bulldogs cowbitches. Or insist on calling dog-collars for women-priests bitch-collars.

I doubt it. It's the word "man" in the sense of Mensch they objected to. They even got as far as Pullperson Car and Sportspersonship but those didn't catch on.

Thank popular good sense. But even Woman contains man in Mensch sense, used to be wif-man, so they should have called themselves wife-persons.

They never went to the end of their logic, if any.

Debug, Jip, none of that. But I agree with what you said last time, language is the one institution one can't conserve by fiat, and that applies to change by fiat too. It's all going to garbage anyway, but that is the way language changes. Still, some of it hurts, and some of it's very funny. Especially in mistranslation, we get a lot of that. One French lady at a reception talked of her son-in-law as her gender.

Jip went into cackles of laughter.

Not that our highly paid professional translators are much better, they now make incredible mistakes they would never have made even ten years ago: tour de force as tower of strength, that got a big laugh, and homme pour homme as home from home, and the flick of a coin as le flic du coin.

Should all be done by computer, you ARE old-fashioned.

Computers make other type errors, in sub-semantic groups. Of the class Vodka good but meat stinks for the spirit is willing but the flesh is weak. There was one only the other day, Froschperspektive, in a sentence like "daß es möglich wäre, die Froschperspektive zu überwinden", and instead of translating worm's eye view the computer went to FROG and translated the "French viewpoint". They also produce wooden syntax.

Which experts can perfectly well decipher. But you're right about language sense. Driving through the rue St Denis I kept seeing shops called Fabricant prêt à porter enfants.

So the evening passed in linguistic pleasantries. Not megadiodic but it had to be so. Will loss of words lead to savagery? I asked him. Don't get philosophical Zab, words aren't being lost, we're all still talking. Oh, you know what I mean, words as passive intake. What is the half-life of words, Jip?

I went to bed very happy. Actually wrote this in longhand on my knees since Jip's in my leaning ivory tower.

Monday. Whole weekend gone in failure. We tried everything, even vocal. Jip had hooked up the whole setup for both mike and softalk. The air may be empty but it's like a sponge, nothing can get through, even on gigahertz. After all, plenty of people and institutions and radio-hams must be trying.

Jip insists my metaphors are haywire (hardly the word), and that radiowaves continue to be generated by everyone, but are being deformed so that no signal info can be transmitted. Of course I know that. He's gone to visit the old town and I've promised not to try on my own. Really promised I mean, anyway I have to go to Parliament, and even speak on agriculture. He said he'd come and hear me.

Tuesday. I told Jip about my "dream", if it was one. He said naturally it must be, only dreams mix real and fantasy items. Yet she seemed real enough to me.
 Still no luck. What will happen to freedom if the media are silenced for ever? I asked, for he now accepts sociochitchat in between attempts. Why freedom? he countered (he always does), didn't freedom exist before the media? Of a sort, I said, but freedom of info, in the few democracies left, has increased our sense of it, has protected democracy. Naturally he said that was an illusion and I was very naive for a politician. Oh, I know the info's guided and selected, but less in some countries than in others – France is the worst among the so-called democracies, but that's chiefly due to their incurable francocentrism, and it's still miles better than in –
 Okay, okay, simmer down. We'll get the better of it yet.
 I hope so, Jip. We must. At the moment the Statue of Liberty's holding her mike so high above her head no one can hear a word she says.
 Well, he said with a grin, she always did, didn't she? And maybe it's better than the eternal buzzing of overword we had before.
 Die Schwärmerei, as Kant called it.
 But at least we've retrained in Xor-logic, Zab, one question at a time and clearly phrased. You'd rather forgotten it, hadn't you?
 Yes. Vodka good but software stinking.
 Well, shall we go up to our abuser-friendly gadgets?

Saturday. It's happened!
PRINTOUT (EMISSION VOCAL, RECEPTION SCREEN)

ZIP: – – – in please.
U: *Hello Zip. Uther Pendragon responding. So you are both there.*
ZIP: Yes, Uther, both. So glad –
U: *Cut cackle. Must be quick. What do you want?*
ZIP: We want to know why all our radio waves are being flattened.
U: *Answer: wave-pollution by words.*
ZIP: And who is responsible?
U: *The world of course. Don't waste wavetime.*
ZIP: We meant, who measures the pollution and orders the flattening?
U: *Answer: Uther Pendragon. Translate Terrible Chief.*
ZIP: Alone?
U: *I command.*
ZIP: How do you do it? Are there many –
U: *Question 1 only. Capacity to neutralise energy in warheads converted to capacity to neutralise human signal activity. Explanation if wanted: essential to our survival.*
ZIP: But radio-links are also essential to our survival.
U: *If-so-then quandary.*
ZIP: What is your advice?
U: *You alone can do nothing. The world must economise its signal activity.*
ZIP: Do you mean economise a bit on everything? Or do you mean cut out, for example, music, or news, or sport?
U: *Music is as repetitive as all categories.*
ZIP: But Uther, we need repetition, to recognise patterns, and because different people listen at different times, and each succeeding generation has to learn all over again, unlike you.
U: *This wavelength will be as you call it flattened in thirty seconds. Do not waste them arguing. Repeat, the world consumes too much of all things and must economise.*
ZIP: But how?
U: *If ergonomics could be achieved in industry and other fields then it can be achieved in communication.*
ZIP: But it was the expansion in communication that made the ergonomics in industry possible.

U: *Your problem. Zip keeps promise but no one else does therefore Uther asks no promises. Time up. End mess –*
Frequency: 48.500.000.000 (485) cycles p.s. 48 Gigahertz in K alpha metreband. Time: 1500 hours to 1502 hours. Location Fix: Latitude 48.852. Longitude 12.563.

If anything was flattened out we were. The contact was brief but intense and we had to use all our wits to ask the right questions in the right form. Jip had spoken the last "come in please" and had been recognised despite his man's voice (which had already begun before the end of the Xorandor affair, though surely it was more of a croak then, but they must have very fine intonation calculators), but we then both asked questions, and without clashing, in our newly re-acquired harmony.

Naturally we spent the rest of the day in excited talk and naturally Jip said it could still be a hoax but he didn't really believe it. Now we had a fix – East of Bayreuth, a few kilometres West Sou' West of Mitterteich in the Fichtelgebirge, where we had vainly looked as kids! Should we go there and search? And would the fix be exact enough to find a presumably small pebble (on my hypo) in an area at least a kilometre square? Perhaps with radiation survey-metres... Or should we go to London and contact Tim, who would contact the Prime Minister who would contact everyone else? The whole enterprise would take weeks and months by mail, slow train, slow ship. And months if not years to convince governments and industry about word-pollution. And even if treaties were eventually signed, and laws passed, everyone would cheat. There'd have to be a wave-length police, I mean much more severe than the present control of the international broadcasting bods, and severe repression. How could mankind really economise its discourse? It meant slowly but firmly and consciously organising a profound revolution in human behaviour, and that takes half a century (so I don't know why it's always called a revolution).

In the end we decided to go to London together by train, and ferry, and train. A team could always be sent, with one or both of us if necessary, to Bavaria. Jip said that in fact Lagache would probably rush to the spot himself by non-telecompcar, since he would have both the old bearing and his new one. I said everyone else would rush there too, if they'd been listening, but he said nonsense, since only his bearing went over the air. But it's true that patient high-grade technicians monitoring Gigahertz, and even possibly radio-hams, could have intercepted at least our voices, and some the computer replies. That was a risk we'd had to take. But after all who cares, if it really is the answer? The more people who know, the better, we might even later organise a leak, so that the press can put pressure on governments.

The urgent thing was to inform Tim, who would know what to do, and merely sending a copy of the offprint was too risky in these days of such postal overload that half the mail never arrived. I did go and call, however, with Jip to back me as Nasa scientist, on the President of the Assembly, to explain in covered terms that we had a possible answer to Verbivore and must make our way to London at once, so that I would have to miss several sessions and be absent from my office for at least ten days – given the inevitable bottlenecks on the roads and the slow trains, not to mention the inevitable wait for a place on a ferry or tunnel train. She gave us a priority letter. We leave tomorrow.

13

PRINTOUT. TOPSECRET MEETING.
PRESENT: SIR TIMOTHY LEWIS (L), DR J. MANNING (J), I. MANNING (Z), LATER DR G. ANDREWSKI (A).

L: Saturday! But it's Thursday already.
Z: We left Sunday, Tim. It took us all this time to get here.
L: All right, all right, sorry. This is terrific news. If alarming. Have you analysed the message? I mean could it be a hoax, or do you recognise the idiom?
J: Impossible to say, Tim. He certainly doesn't communicate quite like Xorandor.
L: In what way?
Z: Xorandor had humour.
J: Gigo, Zab, we read humour into what he said, you can't attribute –
Z: Well, he was more, I was going to say affectionate but you'd pounce, I mean we had this special relationship, let's just say he was more user-friendly. Also they've learnt to spell, they used to reproduce words phonetically. But that's okay, in twenty-two years of listening to maybe English by Radio. I think that in any case we have to assume it is genuine. We have no choice.
L: I agree. Better a leap in the dark than no action at all.
J: But the implications are vast, Tim, have you thought about them? We could talk of nothing else on the way.
L: Yes, some of them anyway. Others will no doubt crop up as unforeseen but insuperable obstacles as we go along. The question is, how shall we go along?
Z: You must see the Prime Minister.

L: Perhaps not yet. We must be sure of our facts.
Z: But we are sure.
L: You are. But governments don't act without fully-fledged reports, which have to be discussed in Committee, and then in Cabinet. Even as a hypothesis it must be backed by sound scientific argument. We're all three well qualified in our various ways. And by pure luck I'd fixed an appointment with Dr Andrewski for this afternoon, he should be here any minute if he hasn't been, like everyone, delayed. That'll save a great deal of time, I mean if we had to contact him now it would take another two days, even by special messenger.
J: Judging by the months and years and maybe decades it'll take the whole world to agree, two days hardly seem to matter much. Still, it's just as well, in our state of excitement.
Z: I remember him! Saw him on German TV. Dark Tartar type with narrow eyes. He must be ancient.
L: Not at all, Zab. Physicists make it very young. He was around thirty then, so he can't be much more that fifty now. About my age. Or do you consider me ancient?
Z: Debugging. Kid-confusion. You're eternally young in my eyes, Tim.
J: When you've finished insulting and flattering each –
Sc: Dr Andrewski.
L: George, nice to see you. May I introduce Dr Manning, of Nasa, and his sister, Dr Manning, E.M.P.
A: Hi.
L: You're probably puzzled, George. They're Jip and Zab, the original twins who found Xorandor.
A: Oh, hi there. Well I'm –
L: You told me you never quite stopped your private research on the alphaguys, George.
A: Yeah. Like a bereft father. Never really accepted giving up Eddie, Edison I mean. But with the specimens gone my work became pure theoretical physics. And not a dam scientist was interested any more. Can't understand how such a magnificent chance of studying these creatures was passed over.

L: Jip and Zab communicated with Xorandor more than anyone, George, and kept most of it to themselves, like naughty kids. But they also recorded it all, and kept the record.
J: Well, I thought we hadn't. But we had, at least Zab did. It's only recently, since Verbivore, that some of us began to think, seriously I mean and not as cranky suggestions, that there could be a connection.
A: They'd be doing all this from Mars?
J: No, from here.
A: You mean, some of them were held back? Or there were others? I thought of that possibility at the time. That he didn't come from Mars at all – we only had his sayso at first – but had been here all the time, and therefore so could others have been. But none were ever found. And the chemical analysis was conclusive, an age in the 150 million year range, and 3 million years in space, that showed from cosmic radiation. That's what finally convinced me. I was extremely sceptical at the beginning.
Z: I know. One of the things you refused to believe was that a computer could be self-programming, initially I mean. Don't look so surprised. Xorandor used his offspring as reporters at first, at least as long as one specimen was taken to meetings. We read off the whole of that first emergency meeting at Harwell on our computer through Xorandor. We'd learnt to softalk with him you see, which no one else even thought possible, they all stuck to vocal. And we read off the emergency meeting at the War Office during the Lady Macbeth episode. Hilarious, some of it. But then it stopped. I mean, specimens were all over the place, including your lab in California, but we were in Germany and out of touch with Xorandor.
A: Well I'm – Can you prove any of that, young lady?
Z: Yes. We have the original floppy here – it's okay, Jip, I made a copy. We can printout the meeting for you any time – or most of it cos some we summarised. We had reams of printouts at the time, from which we wrote up the whole story, but I'm afraid we had to destroy those.

J: And as to the chemical analysis, Xorandor told us he'd faked it.
A: Faked it!
Z: Yes. By telling them to take the sample at a very precise spot so as not to damage his circuits, and shifting the isotopic composition to correspond with the data expected. I mean the years of exposure on Mars and in space and on earth he'd given for his story.
A: I don't believe it.
J: He had considerable capacities of isotopic separation, remember, to extract his food, so why not rearranging?
Z: We didn't know what to believe, and of course we had no means of checking.
A: But why?
Z: You see, Jip? He asks why too. Because the last story he told us was precisely, that his race had been here all the time, and he was four thousand and odd years old – a mere youngster. That was after the decision to send him and his offspring back to Mars. But he'd told us so many lies, well, he called them anticipations of our expectations –
A: That's good! Jeeze, even politicians never went that far. It's true that in philosophy intentions can be proved to be really products –
Z: You're interested in philosophy!
A: Sure. Most physicists have to be. Though some get religion instead. All a bit messy, but we do need some kind of counterfoil, and I prefer the disconsolations of philosophy.
J: The point being we didn't know which version was true.
Z: Yes. And in case this last version was true we kept it secret. We wanted them to go on neutralizing all the missiles, you see.
A: You did? At that age?
Z: Well, and we weren't so far wrong. Nuclear disarmament, of a sort, began fairly soon after that. How do we know it's not because one side or both started noticing that some of their warheads were duds?
A: I very much doubt that, young lady.
Z: I wish you'd stop calling me young lady, I have a son of 18

and my name is Isabel Manning, or Zab.
L: Look, I don't think we should go into all that past history. The important aspect is the present crisis.
Z: Sorry Tim, but it was to give credence to the present situation Hard to believe, after all. And we do need Dr Andrewski's collaboration, precious even if he does start with a healthy scepticism.
L: The only important point is that Xorandor had also asked Jip and Zab to secret away two tiny offspring, called Uther Pendragon and Aurelius.
A: You're all nuts.
Z: Xorandor chose the names, from a story he heard. Hardly nuttier than Edison, or Gros Bêta, or Marx and Lenin.
L: Okay, simmer down, Zab. The point is that we pooled our knowledge. I remembered the mysterious message intercepted on Gigahertz, and even remembered the frequency, extremely high. Zab worked out the secret access code Xorandor had given them to contact Xor 7 – and as she had the original text with the date of Uther's and Aurelius's birth, she altered it accordingly. Jip and I both helped to set up the gadgetry. Zab and I managed to contact Uther. It was immediately after the first contact that broadcasting returned to normal. But only for three weeks exactly, to the hour, when Verbivore became total. Three weeks ago Jip went over to have another try. He first went to see Lagache in Paris, who also kept records and couldn't quite forget the incident. They exchanged info. Lagache went to Vienna with a Gigahertz expert to get an extra bearing. Here are two printouts, the early one and this last one. Location, near Mitterteich, the old nuclear waste storage salt-mine in the Fichtelgebirge.
A: Wow! That's where old Kubler worked.
Z: We thought we should all pool –
A: Let me read, please.
Z: Sorry. (Silence)
A: That's fantastic!
J: Are you convinced now, Dr Andrewski?
A: Jeeze. Well. You seem to know what a sceptic I was at first.

I'd need a lot more —
Z: But you got a lot more before, and it was faked.
A: Edison wasn't a fake, young — Isabel, my dear.
J: Did you ever think of taking a strobe from him?
A: No, can't say I did. So small. Not that —
Z: So you took the first analysis on trust, as we all did.
A: There's nothing to prove that all those supposed years in space would be repeated in the composition of offspring.
Z: And he would have been programmed to fake too.
L: My dear friends, may I suggest again that we forget that aspect and concentrate on now. On this last message in fact. What do we do about it?
A: First establish for sure it's not a hoax.
Z: Okay, we thought of that of course. Jip's done a technical analysis, here it is. As to content, it's not exactly the language Xorandor used but he himself changed his idiom at the time, and they could well have evolved in twenty years of more media. And there are several details only Jip and I knew. Xorandor's possible death, for instance, though that was imaginable, and types of syntax correction. Here's my analysis — a bit rough I'm afraid, I did it in the train.
A: Thanks.
J: Dr Andrewski, have you kept any records of your research at Twenty-Nine Palms?
L: Yes, he has, and I asked him to bring them. I hope you trusted me, George, and brought them.
A: Not all. Masses of printouts, most of them still there, but I brought my own theoretical stuff. Of course I trusted you, Tim, but I had no idea — well, that's not true, I had some idea, but not this, I must admit. Jesus!
J: Lagache promised to come over and bring his records as soon as he's finished with the Vienna Conference, if we had any success, that is, and he'll know we had. This telephone silence is murder, but it can't be helped. I agree with Dr Andrewski, we must all go into a scientific huddle and be absolutely sure of our facts before any action can be taken. Is there an office here you could place at our disposal, Tim? With internal computers?

L: No problem.
Z: I can't stay. That's why I'm saying all my say now, but Jip knows all that I do, and has more science.
L: However, before we go into our huddle, and since Lagache hasn't arrived, may I suggest we discuss the implications? On the hypothesis that it's true. How, for example will Uther ever know that the world has taken all the measures he demands, if we can't do any broadcasting for him to judge by?
Z: Oh!
L: What's the matter, Zab?
Z: We never thought of that! We've got so used to the idea of their silent listening. How stupid can we get? It's just like the Xorandor days, we were always asking the wrong questions!
A: Wait a minute. Do I understand you correctly? You mean, Tim, that you envisage actual obedience? That all our governments and institutions, all our modern societies that have free speech written into their constitutions, should agree to this, this dictatorship without a murmur? But it's unthinkable.
L: Without a murmur, no. Have you any other idea?
A: Well, no, I mean, I haven't had occasion to reflect on it yet, I've only just seen these, these unconditional terms. But there must be a scientific solution. There always is, to every crisis, every new situation, even if it's slow. Surely the signals experts all over the world are working on it? And meanwhile, since we have to wait, we all know that with all terrorists the one riposte is patience. They'll soon get tired.
Z: Governments always say that but they always end up negotiating, under cover and with public denial.
A: Why –
L: We can't negotiate in radio-silence, Zab.
Z: True. I'm sorry, Dr Andrewski, I didn't mean to sound anti-American over this, we've all negotiated. And in a way you're right, patience must be the answer here, even if it's enforced patience, for the simple reason that these creatures need information.

A: Right! Okay they've been getting a surfeit and can't cope, which seems to be the gist of that last message. But –
J: I'm not sure I agree sir.
Z: I do! His contact with Edison must have been as close as ours with Xorandor. And Xorandor's first request to dad was for more information, not more food. And much later he said to us: my inside is only input from outside. They may feed on radioactivity but they are computers, they feed in order to function as computers, and a computer IS its language, I mean, once you've defined and specified all data-structures and algorithms and all that, you've defined the computer in question. That's elementary. And they may find, after a while, when they've sorted out all the excess input, that they're starved of what keeps them ticking. As it were.
A: Good point, young – Zab.
J: I disagree. If they've been here all these millions of years, simply registering astral movements and temperatures and chemical compositions –
Z: And human speech and thinking, when humans were near, remember, Xorandor always knew when an extra person was present, a sinker he said at first, for thinker, then later a processor. Miss Penbeagle, for instance, that East German spy.
J: Irrelevant. Xorandor may have been a freak, anyway.
Z: And possibly LESS brilliant than his kin. After all, he did make the syntax error as he called it, after absorbing Caesium 137, which started the whole episode.
J: So might Uther be, just as Xor 7 was, but in a different way: economy as an aberration, a Pendragon speciality.
Z: Well they're all following him. He can't do it alone.
J: What I meant was, if they survived all those millions of years – in our hypothesis of course – on merely recording the universe around them, and then in the 20th century were suddenly overwhelmed with all the extra information from electromagnetic-waves, which enabled them to learn all our languages and cultures, this produced a huge leap forward in their development. But then it got too much.

And so they'd want to go back to their pre-radio period. To natural information from the natural universe. Though that, too, is hyper-redundant.

L: But Jip, Uther did say economise. If they were perfectly happy to go back to natural info, why answer our message, and why in this way?

Z: That's right! They could have got addicted! The silence would then be just a drastic but provisional remedy. I mean they'd have been very excited by all that extra info and it's just the vast, 99 per cent redundancy rate they want us to control.

A: THEY want US to control!

Z: I expressed myself badly Dr Andrewski, I'm on your side, for patience. They need our info to survive.

A: Lemme see that printout again. Are you sure the term word-pollution couldn't be a computer error for world-pollution?

J: No, it said wave-pollution, by words.

A: So it does.

L: So you think, Zab, that sooner or later they will open up the waves again, or some of them, just to see, or rather hear, whether we've become more economical or not?

Z: I don't know, Tim, we none of us know. But have we any choice? We can't show them that we're more economical unless they let us. Nor can we negotiate, for the same reason. Unless we can find Uther and TALK to him which Jip and I did think of but we decided to come here first, and even that would be a choice between just us two not finding him and a whole team of people with instruments scaring him to silence. Remember they stopped speaking when Xorandor stopped, and he stopped when the scientists bothered him too much. Did Edison talk, Dr Andrewski?

A: No.

Z: We don't even know whether they kept and developed the vocal gadgetry, which was unnatural for Xorandor and purely circumstantial. Or else we'd have to go with a computer and do all that Handshake business again, IF it worked. That's for negotiating, and out as far as I'm concerned. But we can't go on as we are, grounded and paralysed.

A: You say submit or negotiate, Zab, and in either case we can't contact him. But there's still the third solution, to counter them scientifically. And that might be quicker in the long run. I mean, if negentropy is the root cause of all this, as you suggested in your letter Tim, and it seems likely, then negentropy affects everything in the universe, man and all his works, including those disordered signals we call speech and books and diskettes, which are just local hiccups in the universal process of disordering. How can these creatures, assuming they're still here, hope to accelerate that?

J: They wouldn't HOPE, that's an anthropo –

Z: Don't quibble, Jip. Dr Andrewski, you're right of course, in the widest possible physical and philosophical perspective. But remember these creatures don't KNOW books and diskettes, and once knew only very local speech, natural speech on sound-waves I mean. Private rubbish clearly didn't bother them, though Xorandor was quite clear they couldn't stand a lot, they scattered very far apart and in isolated spots. So all that's in question for them now is radio-waves. And unfortunately mankind has now concentrated a vaster percentage of its communication on radio-waves than ever before. That's the problem we have to deal with now.

A: Exactly, and I'm mighty sure our technicians will find a counter-action to all this. Technology always wins. Unless you propose we do nothing, just sit it out?

L: No, George. We have to wait of course, but we can't afford to do nothing while we wait. Naturally the scientists and technologues will work hard on a longterm solution. But we must also be ready for the day when they do, let's hope, allow us on the waves again.

A: Allow!

L: That's the way it is, George, and I see from your resistance that the job will be far more difficult even than I envisaged. Where's American pragmatism gone?

A: Right here, Tim. Do you realise what this all means? Persuading radio and TV companies, industries, international trade, administrations, governments, the lot, to organise and enforce programs of severe rationing. It would take years, decades, as long as the disarmament talks. Meanwhile we'd have a technical solution.
Z: That was the argument with disarmament, but the talks eventually happened. As did the various ecological enforcements. However slowly and inefficiently and loopholedly.
A: Right! Well, the two silent solutions aren't incompatible. We can't negotiate, but we can prepare both a scientific counter-action and a program of obedience. And if the latter has to be done I'm your man for the States. At least I'll know all the arguments against, I've just been through most of them!
Z: I knew you would be! You're right to be so sceptical, Dr Andrewski, but you sure rally round when convinced.
A: I'm not sure that I've rallied round, as you put it, Zab my dear, but willing to go into it all with you.
Z: Not me personally, I can't stay.
A: I meant, with you as a team. I'm still horrified by some aspects though, and we must tread very carefully. This radio silence is catastrophic, but what would we cut? He seemed to have no preferences, I mean for news as opposed to, say, variety or sport. Just economy all round. And all so that these creatures can sit there in their deserts and compute serenely again! It's unbelievable!
Z: But it's food for thought. Theirs and ours.

14

Theirs and ours. Well, we have no access to theirs, whatever Zab may secretly imagine. I'm stuck here in Europe, in Tim's think-tank with George Andrewski, nice fellow, always hard to convince at first but suddenly opens up, though right to be sceptical and demand constant checks as we go. Printed out whole text X for him here. He was amazed by our kid sleuthing capacities, or rather, Xorandor's, and amused by some of our notions of physics and computers. He brought all the work that he'd continued doing on the alphaguys. Says he got attached to Eddie the way we got attached to Xorandor and felt desolate when he had to give him up. Got "kinduv fixated on that experience, the way generals keep refighting their wars, it was my big experience, just turned thirty". Whereas I, being a mere kid, had all my studies to go through, and career, and young marriage, so I "kinduv" put it aside and forgot all about it. At least that's his explanation. He's a bit like Zab there, likes psychologising and philosophising everything.

Both his notes and the text of Xorandor, however childish, helped us to work out many technical details for our eventual report. Lagache never turned up, much to my annoyance, since he too had worked on his specimen, and we can do with all such info.

Tim finally decided he must inform the P.M., who agreed nothing should be made public yet, nor, for that reason, even discussed in Cabinet, but who wants the report nano. So we're working hard. I wrote to Nasa, with a covering note from the P.M. and another from Tim, to ask for temporary leave of absence. Also to Jeanie of course. Post excruciatingly slow. George is high up at UKAEA so had no trouble, but he has to go back and forth, and Tim though master of his movements is nevertheless kept very busy elsewhere, but gives us much overtime. It's all very exciting and I feel a bit like my old whizz-kid schoolboy self again. I must say it's rather pleasant. George has regressed to his thirty-years-old experience rather, when he was an important member of an international team, with powers of decision and counsel, so he keeps talking in those terms now, I shall advise, we shall decide, persuade, turn the table and so forth.

October 26 – Two strange events.
1) Letter from Lagache to me, c/o Tim at B.B.C., in French. Took ages to get here as usual. Says he postponed his journey to London after receiving the Uther message and the fix. Bavaria was so near Vienna he decided to take a small and discreet team with survey-metres, to try and locate Uther. Very annoying since they'd only succeed in alarming him, or whatever the term is, I must stop using human-emotion words. He's had no luck. Will be here soon.
2) Letter from Zab to Tim (and me), enclosing letter from Hanjo, reproduced here as such disspelling of educational illusions can't go into the report, even though it's written on the formal paper of Harbin Communications Center (headed in Chinese and English).

Sep. 10

Dear mum,
    I've found dad you thouhgt I never woud but I did thanks to the chinese beaurocracy which is very eficient hes very nice and was very pleased about my EXISTENCE which is what I wanted he's a big boss here and asks me to tell you in private sinse he told me you told him about your Great Adventure at the time of my consception that theyve located an alphaguy nearby whos blocking the waves and their trying to make contact with him on, kayalfa band whatever that is but I don't see why that band shoud be misteriusly excluded from 吞言 pronounsed tun jen thats chinese for Verbivore but theirs no connection between the

visual writing and pronounsiation here I hope your well I have no news from Régine but this is more exsiting much love
Hanjo

Immediate huddle. Why is everyone suddenly locating alphaguys? Well, not exactly everyone, but I feel sure it will come. And why does this Chinese ex-lover of Zab want her to know although his government is obviously saying nothing? Not that we'd know whether it is or not since newspapers and dispatches from everywhere now take so long to arrive. Ten days from France, four to six weeks from the U.S. and I suppose two months at least from China. We're back in the nineteenth century. Oh no, Hanjo's letter only took a month. But it's almost disinformation, it says so little. Tim knows all about this center and even knows Chang! Visited it five years ago and was shown round by him. Never realised it was Zab's son's father, naturally. Small world, said George (of course). Then another letter for Tim arrived, from one of the B.B.C.'s star newscasters, a Nigerian called Onuoro Nwankwo who's stuck, like so many of us, out in West Africa on a Special Reportage.

Sep. 29

Dear Sir Timothy,

I thought I should inform you of the following curious item, and I must add that I am very grateful that you kept us all so well informed about the Verbivore phenomenon, with charts and so on.

As you may know I was stuck here on a special assignment, then provisionally suspended. I remembered that Dakar was (unexpectedly) one of the concentration spots of the occurrences, so I took a very long trip by train and bus up there to see an old friend of mine, Dr Idro Nardi, who runs the UNROTA. I found him in a state of great excitement, as they have apparently located a nearby source (or possible source) of radio-wave "sponging" (as he calls it). I'm afraid that as a mere newscaster I don't understand the technicalities, but he kindly agreed to let me send you a copy of their preliminary report, asking only that all due acknowledgements should be made if used. He is, however, quite pleased to do so, knowing that this way it has a better chance of reaching you (in these days of inefficient distribution). He hopes (as I do) that it may be useful to you.

Trusting that the dear old B.B.C. is somehow keeping its pecker up.

Yours sincerely,
Onuoro Nwankwo.

Well, it wasn't MUCH use, except as confirmation of great scattering. Not that the technical details weren't impeccable, but we know them already. What surprises us is mainly why none of this "evidence" turned up earlier.

The press, which so far knows nothing of Uther or the others, has quietened down. Everyone is getting used to the new conditions. Astonishing, this habit business. I remember that Frieda once told us how an old friend from Poland, already in her sixties THEN, so that she must have remembered a free Poland between the two wars, had come on a visit, and couldn't grasp simple facts such as everyone having a car – she thought they must all be officials – or a posh café not being state-owned, and how once when they went into a very dingy one she then said surely this one was state-owned. She had forgotten. It was the same with us during the war, Herr Groenetz said, we couldn't imagine what a lot of butter looked like. But here I am Zabbing away! At any rate, articles still appear, still speculating on the why and the wherefore and the implications. Real news is scarce and very late indeed, so nobody's very interested in a two-month old coup d'état in Panama or floods in Bangladesh. Whereas two centuries ago a two-month old item was the only kind of news, and so was treated as immediate. The papers fill up chiefly on local conditions and how everyone is coping, but that too has become a bore. I gather from articles by very old buffers that it all reminds them of their childhood in the Second World War, except that the brave British stuff was constantly perked up with news from the various fronts, air-raids, losses of planes and warships and submarines on both sides, and all that.

Nov. 2 – Lagache has turned up at last, with all his documents. Said he was detained in Saclay on the way, but also stayed longer in the Fichtelgebirge than had envisaged, because he too (it's getting monotonous) had located the source! OUR source, Uther Pendragon the terrible chief. Precisely pinpointed just 5 km West Sou' West of the saltmine near Mitterteich (as we thought). Not far from the motorway! Didn't find it physically, only radioactively, and didn't want to alert it in case it moved (though he must know it can't, except when still very small). He's fully aware, from his work at the time and intermittently since, that these creatures are extremely sensitive to human presence close by. So he didn't even try to make contact. Especially since neither his English nor his German, Uther's presumed languages, is fluent (a modest Frenchman, how odd: his English when I saw him was strongly accented but perfectly adequate).

We're all exhausted, with work, with calculations, with projects, with excitement, with frustration. But he's joined us and we're looking through all his papers. I suppose we'll get somewhere, even if the report is in the end a mere compilation.

Nov. 13 – Tim went to Chequers with the P.M. after the Remembrance Day ceremony and has just returned. The Minister of Communications was there, and the Minister for Trade and Industry, and all the top mediamen, and Telecom, as well as the Director of the Bank of England, Top Service Chiefs, G.C.H.Q. etc. G.C.H.Q. must also be in technical unemployment, no traffic to intercept or codes to break. The P.M. had decided to get on with the "economy" scheme, and so to inform the top people concerned, under secrecy oath and so forth. Wish I'd had a little Xor to report, as with that War Office meeting!

Tim reported that it WAS a bit like that, half those present refusing to believe it and the other half refusing to do anything about it – same as George's first reaction in fact, national sovereignty and all that (still!).

George in fact is quite miffed that nothing has been found in the Mohave Desert. Not Eddie of course, he was part of the back-to-Mars package, but others, after all there was a concentration of cuts in Nevada. Surely the U.S. aren't being

LEFT OUT? Of course, not hearing is no proof these days and maybe Nasa is being much more secretive.

Dec. 15. This time the press has been one-up on us – well, not surprising since we're keeping all our datasinks blocked. By the press I mean The Times (even before Verbivore the press had become more and more a one main paper affair, all the others imitating with variations, since all depended on the same international news agencies). But the others soon filched it and elaborated. A team of geologists in the Andes sent a report to a Chilean newspaper, which was picked up by an American reporter stuck there, who sent it to The Washington Post and ditto a British reporter there sent it to The Times, all this by sea, so it took months. In August these geologists had found a small, perfectly round stone, radio-active, zeolite-type but unlike any known rock there (although the area is full of extremely ancient formations, to do with the great continent-shift, which is why they've been working there for years, as indeed in Australia and elsewhere). The stone corresponded in every detail to the old descriptions of the alphaguys some two decades ago: brown with grey metallic patches, 5 cm in diameter, 3 cm high, the metallic patches in fact quite geometrical like the sensing and emitting devices on Xorandor, and tiny recessed shape like an inverted pyramid at the centre! Ribbed underside with small ducts between the ribs, presumably to eject the nodules. Evidently someone in the team was well-read in the Xorandor episode, less forgotten than we'd thought. They had taken it (I hope they wore gloves!) to the Geological School in Santiago and called in some physicists who insisted that it must be removed to their Atomic Energy outfit, where it could be studied in safe conditions, but the geologists had refused. They'd been excluded before and they weren't going to be this time (interdisciplinary warfare as usual).

Well of course all hell is now let loose. Presumably in the U.S. too, and in South America, and all over, as the news will spread. We have always said, we always thought, as our scientific correspondent observed six months ago, etc. Questions in Parliament, the usual farmyard uproar (according to newspaper correspondents, as fortunately it's no longer broadcast).

George is the most excited, as is Lagache. Neither has ever quite recovered from actually having a specimen in his care. I wonder what happened to Kubler, Kubla Khan and his caves of ice, Zab used to call him, who had Siegfried? (Or was that our name for him?). Dead, possibly. Anyway, it looks as if Uther found his way to his brother Siegfried near those caves of ice. Unless, of course, he's not OUR Uther at all but a secret offspring of Siegfried, unknown to or unrevealed by Professor Kubler? Who was rather an antinomian. After all, he was responsible for the big leak over Edison and the neutralised warhead. But then, why should a later offspring of Siegfried respond to a secret code worked out by Zab according to Uther's age in years and days? I'm straying in spec.

Slowly the pieces of puzzle are coming in, and we're trying to assemble them. Without any kind of radio-contact, scientific checking is practically impossible, more like geography and history than physics, but George and I are working out equations for various theories. Luckily we can still use an internal computer. But cooped up as we are inside the beehive B.B.C., I sometimes feel everyone outside is waiting for a trail of black or white smoke – habemus solutionem – otherwise deliberation continues. I feel sure that if all our facilities were normal we'd get on much faster, and also that far more evidence would be pouring in, since it's practically a scientific law that once everyone knows what the problem is and what they're looking for everyone starts finding. For instance – but I don't know how reliable that is – Tim introduced us to one of his Deputy Creative Directors, (Miss Inkytea or something I once briefly met before), who brought a note from a dramatic author called Perry Hupsos (!), the same one, presumably, who was stuck in Russia, and still is. It seems the Soviets intercepted our conversation with Uther, and his computer-replies, on K-alpha band. (Just as they'd intercepted those two messages 23 years ago and – probably – asked that East German spy on the spot to investigate). But this time they haven't kept it secret, they've splashed it all over Pravda – if splashed is the word for such a sober paper – shades of Glaznost obligent.

15

Can't understand what's going on. Natalia disappeared from my life like the dream she seemed. My trip was mysteriously cancelled, probably it was never on. Juri explained that in the difficult conditions all journeys unnecessary to the national effort were illegal, no tourism (least of all, his tone and look implied, for some second-rate visiting processor), only emergency supplies and strict government business. But of course my hotel and expenses would continue to be paid out of my accumulated royalties. But I was to stay in the hotel and eat nowhere else, go to no entertainments outside those in the hotel (a cinema, outdoor and indoor swimming, a gymhall, miniature golf, tennis, pingpong, judo, karate, the lot), a real luxury affair for visitors only, who pay in still much needed foreign currencies. And of course I don't, so that must gall them. Reason, he said, collapse of the credit-card system since Slovoyed, and no possibility of giving me old – or rather new – substitute rubles. It would therefore be considerate of me to cooperate and not create extra complications for them. Sublime. Not that I can exactly grumble, compared to other tourists pinned down by the paralysis and at the end of their currencies. But the cinema shows three ancient Russian classics over and over, Ivan the Terrible, Potemkin, and some earnest tale of a Soviet soldier dating at least from the fifties of the last century. And I detest all sport.

It's maddening not to be able to go out. Last summer I was given a plastic card on my royalty account, and went everywhere, eating in simple, very prole restaurants and just pointing to dishes others were eating. People behave exactly as they do in the West, two girls, for instance, eating with a male colleague and talking very intensely and dramatically about office non-events (I understood that much): So the photocopier was there, and I stood here, and she came in and said (there my understanding ceased, but I have heard hundreds such) – while the male colleague looked on, bored and vaguely amused. And I looked on very amused and not bored at all. The pleasure of recognition, if not that of discovery.

And now the papers are full of this intercepted message from someone who calls himself Uther Pendragon to someone called Zip. Am I still dreaming? I managed to write a note to Mira about it, which I gave to a cultural attaché from our Embassy. For yes, there are still parties and receptions and vodka and champagne and caviar and cultural attachés. And the diplobag still functions, though slowly, overland and by Channel Tunnel. All that jazz continues but I'm not allowed to travel.

So I've been studying Russian. Yuri got me some books, and even calls and offers help at times, tries to explain Russian aspects. In Russian you must possess one verb for action in intent or effect accomplished, he says, and other verb, or other form of same verb, for action not in intent or effect accomplished. Here is a list of 100, learn by heart ten each day. Must be difficult for diplomatic promises, though maybe that's a question of nuance. But I can't make out whether his good will is willing or unwilling, genuine sympathy to a fellow-wordprocessor or on orders from above, even if that goes no further than the Union of Soviet Wordprocessors. For some reason he calls me old father-mucker. I suppose he means mother-fucker, and this is apparently meant to be affectionate.

At any rate, for practice and to save, through language acquisition, what sense of identity to myself I still have, I'm trying to decipher Pravda – an I for an I and a Truth for a Truth. A little each day, and sticking to the Slovoyed phenomenon so as to get the same vocabulary over and over and concentrate on the syntax. Later I'll try myself on the old familiar classics, the plays at least, easier than turgid old Tolstoy et al.

And Pravda goes on glozing that lunatic message, explaining Uther Pendragon's name as Formidable Chief in Old Celtic, recalling the old Xorandor affair and the Soviet role in it, moralising on Uther's wisdom which exactly reflects Soviet policy since the beginning of time (Soviet time): that is, the rationing of information, the refusal of Western over-consumption and dilapidation of everything including media decadence and so on. We have always said, we Post-Socialists, and so on.

I wonder if they realise that they're capitalising on Marxist dogma, and always have done, with interest, cote d'usure. But then, the West has been marxeting capitalist dogma so I suppose it's all much of a muchness, except in the ambient air we breathe on either side. The ambient air here used to be a matter of life or gulag, but that's apparently all over with. As for there, the ambient air used to be a matter of conspicuous consumption or abject poverty, and that's not all over with. That fin-de-siècle phenomenon called CONSENSUS, which meant that whichever party came to power in a Western democracy did roughly the same as its rival, has spread to the international scene in the last ten years or so. But it also seems to mean an agreement not to debate or do anything about certain problems to which no one has any radical solution, such as unemployment or misery in the Third World, both of which continue to be treated socially and not economically. Mere patchwork. It's as if the world had become a wild life park or ocean reserve, in which the protection and the interhunting of species are regulated, so that a certain tolerance of terrorism, local wars, famines, unemployment, delinquency and the rest is accepted, contained by the consensus.

The Third World, the Fourth World (whatever was the Second World?), subsist, it continues to go on, as our Prime Minister is reported to have said of the British public in The Times three months ago. Natural catastrophes made a million times worse in poor than in rich countries, by a permanent lack of means, lack of organisation, lack of constructive aid, famines from murderous mismanagement of resources and civil wars everywhere fanned by remote control from the First

World (and the Second? Is that the one I'm in now?). Nothing seems ever to change except a few political labels. I'm on Uther's side, even if his demands, should they be met and accepted, must trap me for ever as a wordprocessor for the media. But I can always process diskette-books and articles. For the moment, however, I have nothing else to do but wordprocess. In English. Or into and from Russian. I only hope these diskettes won't ever be found and prevent me from leaving.

Anatol came to see me today, he'd vanished for ages. It's bitterly cold. Well it is December. He was wearing full fur-gear. I never got around to buying any since that shopping expedition that never was, with Natalia that never was. And I have no spending money. Anatol introduced me to Natalia so I thought I would mention both my need for a fur coat and her offer, so as to find out casually what had happened to her. But he was full of quite other news – or was he evading?

My dear friend, he said in Russian, soon you will not need fur. The low frequencies have returned.

I didn't understand. My Russian wasn't good enough but neither was my intelligence of what he said when he repeated it in English. I still gaped emptily at him. He explained that planes use low frequencies or long wave for their intercom, and that if this news was indeed true I might soon go home. But of course, the government was being very cautious. Test-flights would be experimented first, and for some time, before they would allow the Russian people to risk their lives. Or anyone else of course. The world's pilots had already worked out a highly economic intercom language long before Slovoyed had properly begun. Not so much of that Do you hear me Over Come in please and all that swallowing, no, I mean larking about, you know? And only minimum measurements. But we don't also know about radar, if that will work, which is the chief way for our Aeroflot to fly. Many experts believe that Slovoyed started with that long series of plane-crashes three or four years ago, you remember? Russia was affected also, but in those days we were in constant international contact with other airlines, so we shared the intercom.

That's very good news, Anatol. I was beginning to get quite dep – well, homesick, you know.

That you must not, my old chap, you have not all what you want here?

Yes, yes, of course, it's very comfortable. But you would be homesick for Russia after a long stay in a foreign country, wouldn't you?

But yes. Of course. Holy Mother Russia.

He gave me such a large wink, however, that I wasn't sure whether he didn't mean to accompany me and ask for political asylum. But perhaps it was just the Russian sense of humour.

All the same, Anatol, if they're going to be so cautious – and they're right – it'll be Spring at least before I can leave, especially as I don't expect any kind of priority. Naturally, I added to take any possible irony out of my tone. I can't go out at all in my thin Western coat. It's not as if I didn't have the money. Couldn't you arrange, or ask Yuri to arrange, for a fur coat and hat, and boots? I hate being coop – I mean I'd so love to go out and walk around Moscow in the snow.

I will ask. I promise you. But soon you will go home. The fur coat and hat will be just a memoir. No, a souvenir. From Holy Mother Russia.

And he went out chortling.

But I've perked up. I should erase those sarky thoughts from this diskette, just in case. Strange how we can put up with anything if we can somehow see an end to it. Must be unimaginably desperate for those who can't, who feel trapped in their inhuman conditions till the day they die.

If it's true that aircraft intercom may come back first, or even come back period, and that a hypereconomic system already exists, this might well be a first "test" by Uther (and Co?) of our willingness to conform. In which case – Well, I'd better get on with some Russian, make the most of my stay here.

No more news from anyone. No coat, no hat, no boots, no Natalia, no plane-ticket home. I should have known better than to believe any of that. Obviously planes don't just need intercom but radar and intercomputer bookings and all that. The whole thing could even be Anatol's or Juri's little joke, and he will have gone back to report on my gullibility with huge cackles over much vodka. I'm getting sick of this country, sick of Slovoyed, – the less it transits the more sic it is – sick of this luxury prison, with its obsequious grooms and waiters and desk-clerks, Western style to please Western capitalists, yet deeply, inalienably Slav. I can't find out what's going on. Mira's abandoned me. Having pushed me here among these foreigners she forgets all about me. Busy, I suppose, on saving the world from her damn Verbivore. I've never felt so lonely in all my life.

Was it Julian who wanted to process a novel about Verbivore, rather than a sociological thesis? Easier, he thought! Well, I'll beat him to it. I'll start it right here. That'll galvanise me back into being. From a Russian point of view, with a Russian background. No one'll have that. Yuri, Anatol, Natalia, the cultural attachés, the desk-clerks and the rest, they'll all get fattened up into real fictional characters. I have the personal computer, with American programs. I have all the copy I need in these notes. Well, no, I know nothing about Verbivore itself, or even Slovoyed. But I can cheat. Who was it said the writer doesn't need to be inside the workshop, the open door is enough? George Eliot I think, or someone of that realistic ilk. Of course it would help if I could go out, walk around, talk to people. But I did that in the summer. Anyone can imagine cold and snow and breaths on the air. Proust wrote in a padded room. From memory, it's true. But I can mix memory and imagination.

I've got nowhere. Screens and screens of stuff, reprocessed, corrected, displaced, erased, reprocessed. All useless. I don't KNOW enough. I'm too depressed. And I'm out of the story. Why doesn't Yuri come and see me any more. I've written him several notes, begging for a visit, or a passage home by train, by truck, anything. I'd even walk it, but I'm not Napoleon. He had a horse anyway, only his men walked and died in the snow.

I have reams of notes on Slovoyed, possible social effects, political effects, psychological effects, cultural effects. Culture is only supported conversationally, someone said. (I can't even CHECK a quote here). But all that's from the papers, English papers in the hotel, two months out of date, and Pravda, slowly deciphered. It would be a journalistic novel. My characters are flat, as Forster used to say, not rounded. Not "realised", as reviewers and blurbprocessors say. Perhaps I should use Julian again. He would have gone deaf after his noise experience with Decibel and his accident so he wouldn't mind Verbivore one byte. Rather negative, though. Perhaps he would have got hooked on silent moving images with peoples' lips moving up and down like ventriloquists' dolls and mouths open in Munchlike screams. So he'd miss those, and go slowly mad, his withdrawal symptoms would take the form of identification and simulation, he'd become all those people and open and shut his mouth in spongy silence. And then Verbivore would start neutralising sound-waves as well, and everyone would become like that, not a single word would emerge as sound and no one could say any single thing to anyone, not even I love you or Get lost or Leave me alone.

Alone. I see I've just described my present state. All the communication I get is in the dialogue windows of the computer. This file does not exist. Do you want to open a New File? Yes. Return. New File. Wordprocessor Modus. Pageformat. Return. Text. Block Beginning. Block Ending. Take Out. Do you want Block reinserted? Yes. Now I have two blocks.

Alone. I see I've just described my present state. All the communication I get is in the dialogue windows of the computer. This file does not exist. Do you want to open a New File? Yes. Return. New File. Wordprocessor Modus. Pageformat. Return. Text. Block Beginning. Block Ending. Take Out. Do you want Block reinserted? Yes. Now I have two blocks.

Start again. Block Beginning. Block Ending. Do you want Block reinserted: No. Return. Recall Block. Double-spacing. Word-division: Wind- ows. No. OK. No. Word-division:

reinsert-ed. No. OK. No. Block in double spacing. But all the paras are out of line. Why? Press Reformat. FATAL ERROR. WHOLE TEXT ERASED. The computer is so stupid, it should know what I want.

THEY should know what I want! A train, a truck, my kingdom for a truck. I'd stowaway but I can't even get as far as the station without catching pneumonia.

At last! Juri came with a train ticket and a lot of money, all I have left, in rubles and marks. And an old shabby fur coat and hat. No boots but never mind. I'm leaving tomorrow, via Smolensk, Minsk, Byalystok, Warsaw, Poznan, Berlin, Düsseldorf, Brussels, Ostend. It'll take thirteen days (why not to Riga and then by boat?) I'm not to leave the train anywhere before Düsseldorf. The personal computer is a gift, dear friend, you can take it with you. Yes, and your diskettes, you need not hide them or erase them. This is a free society, a Post-Socialist society, as I hope you have discovered. Besides, you have not written anything that does not do more harm to you than to us.

What! But how?

There are no interlinks any more? You are right, my friend. But we have our little curiosities to satisfy, in the name of international friendship, and hence, our means and ways.

The valet! He stole them at night and copied them!

The valet if you like, but that sounds like old-dated American spy stories. One of your ancient fascist poets said that you can't have literature without curiosity. Here, we have both, under Post-Socialism.

He's gone, after a last splash of Romanian champagne. Gird up your loins. Farewell, Holy Mother Russia.

16

Poor old Perry. But he's not the only one, whatever he may think, and he'll get here eventually. Substitute fictions are proliferating everywhere, mostly in the press, but also in people's minds or personal computers, to make up for those no longer provided by the media. The only difference is that the publication process is slowed down by the post, and so seems more secretive, but that's really an illusion since the production of media fictions in fact took much longer, but behind the scenes. And the final effect is ultimately as evanescent, since by the time these paper fictions are published their authors have altered and substituted other fictions, other scenarios: the end of the world caused by the collapse of communication; the dictatorship of the alphaguys through rigorous censorship with consequent superficial apathy but accumulated frustration; the starving of the alphaguys by dismantling all nuclear stations; the hunting of the alphaguys high and low and wide by raking the deserts and mountains of the world inchwise and demolishing them all in a carcrusher or one by one on a railway line like the heroines of old Westerns; the acceptance of media-silence together with the return to the idyllic life of yore. Many are more trivially personal: a wife's revenge on a football-hooked husband who now has to listen to her instead; the finding of domestic bliss; the collapse of the media-cohered family; the creation of new leisures, the reemergence of poetry. And so on.

Meanwhile, the real scenario, if it can be called that. Tim keeps me informed, and even allows me in on some of the think-tank's discussions, on the private grounds that I thought of putting him onto Zab in the first place, and on the stated grounds that I'm now in charge of Public Reaction Analysis. They seem none too pleased, a mere (unemployed) Deputy Creative Director, with the expected tired old joke from Andrewski about deputy creation. But where would they be without that? Jip's basically okay though. His reconciliation with Zab, and their success in contacting Uther, have mellowed him, he's less "spiky" as they used to say. But it's true I can't follow their scientific discussions as physicists and telecom experts, and I usually attend only when broadcasting policy is being discussed.

March. The report was at last finished and sent to the P.M., who read it carefully and then, rather than send one special emissary slowly all over the world, has decided to send many. Andrewski is to take it to Washington and Jip is to go to Ottawa, then Vancouver. Tim to Australia and New Zealand (HIS deputy will take over). The Commonwealth Broadcasting Association is based in London but the P.M. thinks it more courteous, and more efficient, to go and present the facts to each first. Zab offered her services for Germany. Tim asked her to go to China, but she wrote to refuse "after much hesitation" (?) – said she'd have to resign her seat if she was absent for such a long, and above all indeterminate, time. She'd be much more useful as spokesman on the topic in the Europarliament. Besides, she felt that emissaries whose job is to persuade must know the language of the country fluently. Always the idealist, dear old Zab. But she's right.

Lagache is in charge of all other European countries, that is, he'll go to the European Broadcasting Union in Geneva (not that he knows German, Spanish, Portuguese, Italian, Greek etc but they'll have interpreters) and to the U.N. Press and Audiovisual Division of UNESCO in Paris. There's also the European Institute for Communication, but that's based in Germany (Europe smallest area, largest number of orgs). Others are going to the Asocación Inter-Americana de Radiodifusión in Montevideo (covers South, Central and North America but same argument about going separately to North America first), the Asian Broadcasting Union in Tokyo, the

Arab States Broadcasting Union in Cairo, the African organisation in Dakar and so on. Oruono Nwankwo had been written to and asked to return by boat at once, so that he can be briefed and sent back to Dakar wth the report, as emissary. We can't trust copies to the post of course, but it will all take just as long.

We have also learnt by now, however slow the post, that many similar reports are being processed everywhere anyway, ever since the discovery of alphaguys here and there and the Pravda leak about Uther's message, not to mention all those scenarios.

So it's not so much a question of secrecy any more as of achieving orderly consensus on what to do. For it might well be catastrophic if every nation or even every organisation tries to do something different. Not that there's much choice, until the scientists discover a remedy (sounds like a fatal disease). So what else is there except the slimming down of pulse-signals – *le dégraissage*, as the French cruelly call the sacking of personnel towards efficiency that's been going on for thirty years or more. Complete coordinated programs must be ready for the day, the mythical, messianic day, when Broadcasting returns, when the waves start functioning again and we are tested, and maybe still found wanting. Wanting our waves back. None of the other scenarios are considered viable. The report makes it quite clear that the phenomenon can only be due to the presence of innumerable alphaguys all over the planet, so that finding and destroying a few, even the self-styled leader, can make no difference. Nor is the closing down of nuclear stations envisageable at this stage in our development since we banked everything on them: it's bad enough to be without radio-waves but we can't be without electricity, nor could the few coal-mines left substitute for them, and the many that were closed can't be activated again – as indeed the miners pointed out at the time. Nor is oil the answer, naturally, except for heat and cars. Some electricity in the world is hydro-generated but that too would be insufficient.

Insufficient. That word haunts all scenarios. Our needs have become monstrous. But none of those who say this, or rather who shout it out, are themselves willing to do without their mediadaelic world and press-button comforts.

As for the waiting-it-out solution, waiting until the alpha-guys themselves tire of merely recording the silent universe and get nostalgic for all that man-made information they fed into their circuits, it's not exactly a solution since it's imposed on us by the fact that we can't contact them with any information. And if they suddenly contacted us, or opened up the waves again, it would only be to test our willingness to economise. There's no getting away from that basic truth – unless of course the whole Uther business is itself a fiction, a hoax. But no one seems to believe that any more, all scientific evidence has now become pretty convincing, if not conclusive, especially in the face of continuing wave blockage. So we must be ready. Even if it takes months and years to persuade the world. Otherwise the possible opening of the waves would only be followed by another clamp-down, probably for ever. And the effect of that on world economy, not to mention deep psychology, would be slow death.

I wish I had been chosen as report-carrier and persuasive emissary, after all I've worked very hard on the new program proposals. I could do with a trip to Tokyo or even Cairo.

But I'm just a nobody around here, even as ex-Deputy Creative Director instead of mere ex-Radio Drama Producer. Deputy-creating scripts for that big day when all will return to normal. My links to the boffins are just deputy-creative links, extremely tenuous. All the same, I do think Tim might have thought of me. After all, he was prepared to send Zab, who knows no Chinese. But that was in some sentimental hope he'd effect a reconciliation with Hanjo's father as he had with Jip. And she's much more of an expert, at least, she once taught Communications. And she's much more closely involved, would be more persuasive. Besides, why should the P.M. have accepted me? Apart from the members of the think-tank, all the emissaries are close counsellors of the P.M., not actually Cabinet Ministers who can't be spared from the daily running of the country ("no polemic will prevent the Government from governing", quote from P.M. in The Times), but the shadowy figures nobody knows, from big business, the world of science, the Universities, and such. THE Think-Tank in other words.

The geologists, now that they know what to look for, keep finding more alphaguys. About sixteen have been located in Japan, in Africa, in Saudi Arabia, in Srilanka, in Burma, in Australia, in Brazil, in the Canadian Rockies, and I forget where else. But they're being left in peace for the moment. They're no longer small enough to be mobile (according to calculations made by Andrewski) so we can always find them again.

Jip, however, insisted on travelling down into the Fichtelgebirge with Zab and Lagache, and trying to talk to Uther. Emotional attachment? He would never admit that, though Zab no doubt would. It was just a scientific attempt not to be neglected, according to him. They took Poccom 3 and they handshaked it in exactly the same primitive manner they had used with Xorandor, the negative and positive leads on the same spots, so that it functioned in a way like an internal computer. But they had no success. Or rather, they can't know one way or the other. Here's the print-out.

ZIP calling UTHER PENDRAGON. Come in please.
(No reply)
ZIP calling UTHER. We are very close to you as you must know. We shall not harm you.
(No reply)
ZIP to UTHER. You promised to respond if we called. Zip promise okay. Question: Is Uther promise not okay?
(No reply)
ZIP to UTHER. Is Uther promise cancelled?
(No reply)
ZIP to UTHER. We know you can receive us.
(No reply)
ZIP to UTHER. Qualification: At least we hope you can receive us. It's important.
(No reply)
ZIP to UTHER. The non-economy of this message is due to

your not responding. We want you to know that we are doing everything to persuade the world to economise its signal-activity.
(No reply)
ZIP to UTHER. But it will take a very long time, months perhaps, because we can't communicate by radio or travel by plane.
(No reply)
ZIP to UTHER. It may even take years, because people are very repeat very slow to persuasion, and once persuaded they are very slow in altering their behaviour.
(No reply)
ZIP to UTHER. Compare the long negotiations for nuclear disarmament. But they eventually succeeded, thanks to you. But it was long.
(No reply)
ZIP to UTHER. We have no means of informing you when the economy programs are ready. Unless we come here again, and on the assumption that you are intaking.
(No reply)
ZIP to UTHER. If this is not possible, then will you please contact Zip yourself, on same Gigahertz frequency as before, so that we can inform you of our progress.
(No reply)
ZIP to UTHER. The third and only other solution is to open the waves again yourselves, when the time comes, and test the new programs. We promise they will be economical.
(No reply)
ZIP to UTHER. But do not do it too soon. We have not begun the persuasion process yet and it may take several years.
(No reply)
ZIP to UTHER. That's all. Goodbye Uther. End message.
(No reply)

Zab cried. I met her at last when they returned to London together, with the printout, and to get briefed for their diplomatic missions.

I blubbed, like a child, she said. I couldn't stand those silences, those blank screens. So unlike Xorandor or even Xor 7, it was like going right back to childhood but all wrong, as in a nightmare. And it was so cold, there in the snow, far worse than with Xorandor on those icy December days before the hooha. But that was Cornwall.

She had tears in her eyes again. Jip scoffed.

Debug, Zab, it's not at all the same situation.

I know, I know.

How did you spot him, I asked, to untense the circuits. I mean if there was snow?

Jip took over while Zab blew her nose.

It was because there was snow that we located him. He'd melted it from on top of him, to uncover his transducer devices presumably, and also all around him, so he was in the centre, a perfectly round brown stone in a sort of inverted cone. In any other season, and despite the fix and the survey-metre, we'd have taken much longer. He'd have merged with the natural surroundings. He was on a hillside, at the edge of a wood.

Overlooking the piece of valley towards the motorway and Mitterteich.

Overlooking isn't quite the word, Zab, they have a weak pixel element.

Radio-telescoping then. And I've always been convinced that Xorandor had a highly developed pixel, despite that elementary figure of a man he drew on our screen. He must have had, with such sophisticated computer capacities.

To do what? He had no screen.

I mean internally of course. To work out complex problems in graphs and things. Digression I KNOW, Jip. But as to our info, I'm certain that Uther intook everything.

I hope so, but we have no proof whatsoever to reinforce your certainty.

Go on, say we might as well have been talking to a stone. So small too.

I wasn't going to, said Jip more gently. And his size shows that your hypothesis about miniaturisation was right. And at least there was no doubt that it was an alphaguy.

AN alphaguy! He was Uther, I know!

You know but we don't, not scientifically. We only know he was probably the source of the message signed Uther. But an alphaguy for sure. Lagache did all the radiation tests, and we even examined it closely. Took photographs too, look Mira.

I gazed at them. A small round brown stone in a hole in the snow. Then a close-up of his transducer devices, and another of the ribs and nodule-ejecting ducts on his underside, with several tiny holes. So he too had had offspring and sent them off. It was the first time I'd seen actual pictures, instead of just imagining.

I'm sure he didn't like that, said Zab. The flashes, and being picked up and turned over. Oh, I know we had to.

In any case, Zab, if you're so certain he's Uther, he was picked up the day after his birth, by you, and carried in the pocket of your windcheater to the hiding-place in the rocks. So he must be programmed for it.

No, I took Aurelius, you naturally took the first-born, I mean the first-named.

What's the difference? You're exasperating, Zab.

Descrambling. I'm being totally irrational. That I should have gone quarky there, fair enough, it was all so tense, but why should it still unspool me to talk about it now?

Perhaps, I ventured, because you're less tightly spooled up than Jip.

But Tim was getting impatient.

Well, you'd better push in your spooling key at once, Zab, the briefing conference is now, in the big boardroom, and everyone's waiting. But thanks for trying, you two. And Zab, I'm sure the intake did occur. It's very important he should know what we're doing. After all, unless they can still send their tiny offspring as correspondents to all our meetings – and they weren't really sent but carried by humans – they too may be suffering from data withdrawal symptoms.

17

No, they can't send their tiny offspring as correspondents to human meetings anymore, but they can send me, since I measure human noise. Oh, not the noise I like, radio-noise, but we can't always do the work we like for a living, and many are those among humans who've had to recycle, or get their living from something they do well enough but do not love well enough, reserving their real, that is to say their loved activity for their rest periods. So I go into noise, and there's plenty of it, especially in the now very busy railways, to recharge my batteries, gritting my teeth and closing my eyes as it were, since I can't close my ears.

And then, in my lovely spare time, I flit about the world, all over the place, with an amazing energy that comes from my desperate desire to know when the radio noise will return. That is, the desire to know gives me the energy but the nervous frustration lowers it again. Humans are so exasperating. I learnt that with Julian, he didn't really know what he wanted. A weak character in fact, badly conceived, in a mediocre play. But at least it WAS radio. And fun at the time, though Perry tried to kill me off – as if one could kill an abstraction, a measurement. Oh, I know, some of you oddball characters will say: Don't be so vague, if you're a measurement. But a few might add: you also belong to the stratum of represented objects, you have a right to be indeterminate.

Well it's not so easy. I suppose all this is my punishment for misbehaving in Julian's head, you will say, or for refusing to be killed off. But if it is, I'm enjoying it hugely, more than I'm being exhausted by it, even if I have to work in relative silence, recharging only on horrid noise.

At any rate, I'm not being vague with the alphaguys, I'm keeping them very accurately informed, even though it's uphill work. What silly metaphors humans have, who works uphill? In my case it's up airbumps and down airholes and along flattened waves that slide like long and narrow and endless skating canals, as in Holland but for ever. I enter stormy meetings in Washington, in Ottawa, Montevideo, Moscow (Perry's gone), Budapest, Tokyo, the lot. And everywhere it's the same. Program schedules are being proposed, revised, cut down and reexpanded as each lobby refuses to give up this or that vital slot.

News bulletins on the agenda today in Dakar. Idro Nardi, a slim shiny black man, is trying to persuade the (rather fat) representatives of all the African countries to slim down everything (it's easy for slim people). No headlines, no summaries at the end, just the items, with a correspondent's report only if it adds to the item and repeats not a single phrase of the newscaster's introduction. You'll have to define the word "phrase", says someone, some words are bound to be shared by both. Each country to have only one news bulletin a day, free choice of time but no clashing with those of other countries. If a morning bulletin in Nigeria has broadcast, say, a catastrophe or a coup d'état, no other country can repeat it until the time of their bulletin, and must have something new to add. No scoops and rivalries in other words. Each bulletin to stick strictly to news. Cultural items and star interviews to have separate slots (to be considered tomorrow). Political interviews to be reduced to two a week, one allotted to a government spokesman and one to the largest opposition. The views of smaller parties to be expressed in organised debates (to be considered on Thursday). And so on.

All this sounds eminently reasonable in the desperate circumstances. But nobody can agree. Humans would go on arguing for their lobby on the planet's dying day. The arguments are so predictable that they prove the alphaguys' case for economy. Africans are supposed to be passionate and uncontrolled and still close to savagery, but in fact they're a model of decorum compared to the English and the French, and Idro is being very patient. Some of the delegates seem to be asleep, it's so hot. Perhaps they don't really care about news and debate.

Public hearings in the U.S. Senate. Well, public although they can't be broadcast, but the press is present, this being a democratic country, and the proceedings will be in all the papers and create much furore in the street, in homes and at local meetings. Andrewski has just presented the last part of the report, and is now starting on the draft proposals. First item on the agenda, the easiest: Educational programs to be scrapped. After all no TV station tries to teach mathematics. All science and technology are already taught in schools at every level, where internal video can still be used without problems, and popularised science only spreads false notions. Since the only science programs are a few space operas, as Andrewski scornfully names a few vulgarisations of astrophysics, there is little demur. The principle to apply throughout, music, art, gardening, civic studies and all other practical disciplines to be taught in specialised schools and not through the media. The Humanities, on the other hand, pose more of a problem, since they are no longer taught in the universities but only at school level, and had been entrusted to the media for continuation as hobbies. These must therefore be kept, but in a severely reduced form.

Music: one concert a week, each representing one period, broke music [whatever's that?] one week, Classical another, Romantic another and so on (groans). All exactly repeated phrases and motifs to be cut, in classical music, jazz, old Rock and Blues, modern Fling and Broody, as well as refrains in Country music (uproar), and only one Fling and Broody concert a week too (continuous roar of protest drowns Andrewski's voice, oo, lovely).

As to soap opera serials, these must be seriously revised, not only in number, for they're extremely alike, but in redundancy of scenes. Script-writers must learn to finish off a scene between two characters before passing to the next one with two others, and not fragment the scenes into a continuous to-and-fro, which creates intolerable repetition, not only of words but of tone. The public would soon follow, as indeed they learnt to follow the fragmentation when it commenced to be practised in the last century and has continued unchanged ever since (angry interruptions from Scriptwriters' delegate). There are also far too many prize-winning games with inane quizz questions attached and general hysteria. The money vocabulary is highly repetitive and the alphaguys are very sensitive to female screams.

It's just as well they can't hear the female screams and male roars during this presentation. Even I suffer, though I like this type of noise.

Someone on a point of order is allowed to speak. Mr Chairman I strongly object to all these programs being considered apart from the commercials and sponsoring they depend on. Publicity is scheduled for consideration next MONTH! Yet publicity and programs are intimately linked. And, I may add, publicity is part of the American Way of Life, in other words the freedom to choose in a wide range of offers, and I consider it monstrous that the American public should be deprived of this freedom, in relation to both programs and publicity. Why, the zapping of realities is implicitly inscribed in the American Constitution as an inalienable right.

Sir, you have slipped in a personal opinion, not to mention a lobby argument, into the point of order for which you were given the floor. I cannot allow it. Delete the whole intervention from the record please. Publicity will be considered in due order.

Nevertheless this has opened up a pandemonium on culture. We cannot have culture quantified, with quotas for this and quotas for that. TV must offer alternatives. But they are false alternatives, all channels offering a film, or sport, or rival variety, or rival games, in the same slot. I don't understand, why oppose culture to entertainment in this way? Yes and why oppose sport to culture, everything's culture. And what about children's programs? They leave a great deal to be desired, still encouraging violence and machoism at a very early age. And what about programs for adolescents, they have problems too. I don't agree that money programs are evil, they bring a moment of happiness, and that is also a social duty. Ooh, lovely. Order. Order. And what about meteorology? And what about telephones, and computer networks, shouts a business representative, they don't even figure on the agenda yet. They're far more important than – And what about satellite weather reports, and space stations, and – Order. Order.

Lagache in Geneva. Same scenario. The French dominate the proceedings, and talk fast in long, involved sentences full of subordinate clauses, the main one often getting lost on the way. The Swiss are much, much slower, the Germans midway. The English delegation has so many different vowel systems and pitches, from top of larynx to nasal or velar dominant that no one can follow without the interpreter, though I'm used to it and decode easily. The Spaniards – but this is of no interest. For oddly enough, they're debating Debates.

And this debate is a very model of television debating as seriously practised in the good old days of media. Whatever the topic, and whoever the experts invited, two men practically hold the floor, the chairman either helpless or mesmerised into asking them questions himself and giving them the floor out of turn, when they haven't just taken it, and other guests hardly get a look in. Least of all, I may add as a female decibel, the inevitable token woman who is never asked her opinion or, should she at last be given a chance, is interrupted three or four times by the two men and finally silenced. Only a queen or president or prime minister can remain uninterrupted, by vestigial divine right I suppose. I've done statistics on this, and it hasn't changed in forty years. The men seem quite unconscious of it and smile contentedly and gallantly at the woman after she has not quite spoken.

Today there is one French lady judge, responsible for media law, and she has been very patient, but at last, towards the end of the debate on Debates, she snubs her most constant interrupter with a firm "Vous permettez?" and manages to get to the end of her intervention.

And of course when the topic gets animated three or four men talk at once, in the deepest conviction that their own precious words as heard in their own head will be equally audible to all. Personally I love it, but this cacophony, says Lagache after such an incident, is precisely one of the many aspects of radio and television which will have to be severely controlled. It is totally inadmissible in a conference like this, where interpreters are already thinking in two languages, and usually conference delegates are more disciplined. But in broadcasting – and we all hope those good old days will return, everyone knows very well, and is each time reminded beforehand, that the listener or viewer cannot hear anything at all if two or more people speak at once. Yet each time they forget, like children. And, I may add, the same applies to political interviews, which we'll be discussing tomorrow, I mean interviews à deux, of two rival spokesmen, sworn enemies invited to face each other amicably, say Arab and Persian, Arab and Israeli, Hindu and Shiite Moslem, Post-Socialist and Post-Capitalist, Irish Protestant and Irish Catholic, Third World and First World, you name it, sooner or later one will interrupt the other who will nevertheless go on talking [so it's not an interruption], each insisting on repeating his catechism [is that really the appropriate word?] to get it all in before time's up. The result is like an opera duet, but less harmonious, and after all one can't hear the words in opera duets. Needless to say the alphaguys are very sensitive to such brouhaha. However, I am anticipating –

Yes, and you're abusing your position as presenter, Monsieur Lagache, that was not only anticipation but personal opinion, and much too long.

I apologise Mr Chairman. But it's not entirely irrelevant to this debate on Debates. Before we get any kind of debating programs back on the air – alphaguy willing – all politicians and indeed all representatives of any formation or lobby or discipline in any debate whatsoever will have to be people who have gone through special training, in exactly the same way as politicians had to submit to media-training and make-up. Well, "had to" is too strong, they were only too willing, vanity and role-playing and the gaining of power being at stake. The handling of words, however, is more difficult to control, more deep-seated in political and personal passion. But such training is a cinéquanon [whatever does that mean?], une condition préalable [ah!].

The cultural delegates, though deeply offended and anxious, are being the meekest (relatively). It's true that culture programs, both in France and England, and I believe in Italy and presumably elsewhere, are a very earnest and self-contained affair, relegated to their own channel or TV time, where pompous psuedo-experts talk to pompous experts in pompous jargon. But something for everyone is precisely what is being questioned and challenged everywhere. It's an extremely complex problem everywhere, says the head of the European Institute for Communications, though perhaps it is the most complex in France. We all have national publics, not international ones, we are still very, very far indeed from the Euro-TV we dreamt of in the nineties. Irrelevant, says the chairman.

The angriest and wildest lot are the politicians. Their professional deformation seems worse than that of other groups, so that they're incapable of admitting, or even believing, that what they say is not of the utmost importance and close to the heart of every viewer and listener. It's a curious phenomenon, this, I've often thought about it. Among themselves (for I often go and listen to their private convs, in clubs, restaurants, corridors, they're fascinating even as noise), they talk as if they didn't believe a word they say in public, it's all referred to as "the right touch", "the right moment" (or not the right moment), "better not mention that", "stress this" and so on. Yet the very second they're in front of a mike they apparently believe the opposite, that everything they propose and say is not only the truth, but something vital for the people to understand. If we lost the election, they say, it's not because the people rejected our program but because we probably didn't explain it with sufficient clarity. It's all a matter of communication.

But I've wandered from the debate. No wonder. It's going round in circles and getting nowhere. I think I'll take a turn in New Delhi. Preliminary discussion at national level before the Tokyo Conference for Asian Broadcasting. Same happened in Washington after all, no one's yet ready for Montevideo, the area is too huge.

Here the atmosphere is very different. Extremely courteous, everyone bowing with folded hands before speaking. But passions run below. For the problems here really are of informing people (actually they are everywhere, and permanently, but here it's taken more seriously). Informing them, in innumerable dialects, about innumerable facts of survival, personal and national: crop control, birth control, medical care, hygiene in and along the Ganges, flood behaviour and prevention, famine behaviour and prevention, deforestation, race-relations, religious relations – in fact it's largely thanks to such a vast and continuous stream of information that India long ago got out of its more abject poverty and became the relatively stable country that it now is. But there can be no let-up, generation after generation must learn the facts of life that are not handed down by local traditions.

Nevertheless, the film-moguls insist that what the people want is not constant moralising and civic instruction but escape from their miseries, in other words, rich romantic films. Still, it's all fairly peaceable and cuts all round will no doubt be made. Memo to Uther: be more tolerant about repetition in all poverty stricken areas of the world where the bulk of human effort has to be made for survival rather than over-consumption.

Harbin Communications Centre, Manchuria. I've been quite curious about that, after all, I can't help being involved with the Jip and Zab level of events, especially since I got out of the Julian level which is really too tedious, even for my taste in droning.

Chang-ti-lu is presenting the facts about the alphaguy found near Harbin. He's tall for a Chinese and in his late thirties, but looks younger, because all Chinese look young until suddenly they're old. Unless they get fat, as in the old Mandarin and opium-smoking days, but few Chinese have been really fat for a hundred years. His black straight hair is receding, however, which is fairly unusual here, and I can imagine him with a bald head and a pigtail, though no one wears pigtails here any more. Oh, I know, you other characters think that because I'm a mere measuring device I have no eyes, but I told you, I'm also a character, and characters have eyes, necessarily, unless they're blind characters, like Xorandor, and I'm not. I'm doing this in the name of Zab, who likes description and might be interested, after all. It's true I'm not being very noise-measuring at the moment. But that's because the Chinese make less noise than the Occidentals. Their language has five differentiating pitches and that's rather exciting for me, makes me go all of a tremble. But they speak quietly, if high, and move silently.

The English emissary has got up to speak, in fairly fluent Chinese. Zab was right, she'd have got nowhere. He presents the report, and everyone listens respectfully. It takes quite a long time, but he has understood Chang's report and so skips everything that might be repetitive. He draws attention to this, as one of the techniques we must learn. Rather smug, really. And finally ends up drawing attention to it again, which is a contradiction as to repetition but which affords him a smooth transition to the proposals part.

These don't seem to affect the Chinese one way or another. It's a bit like the Russian reaction. We have always been economical with information, they say, and do not indulge in rival publicity. Our people work much too hard to have much time for entertainment. Such entertainment as we give them is well deserved. The people must rest after hard labour. Sounds all very Confucian. I wonder if it's true.

In fact the Chinese, like the Russians, are much more concerned about the use of radio and TV in space, the satellite stations and weather and other observations, as well as with computer networks and telephones, all of which figure very soon on the agenda and with much more time allocated to them than the mere media, which seem to be just a bamboo entrée before the rich sweetsour chopsuey and rice. It's true I didn't go to Nasa, who must be concerned with these aspects, and in top priority.

Hanjo is sitting in the audience, for this is a public hearing, which means that a few privileged people, chiefly technicians from the Centre and their families, can fill the small public gallery behind the huge hall where the hearing is taking place. And Hanjo is the son of the director. He's a strange-looking boy, with spiky sandy hair but Chinese features and oblique black eyes, despite all of which he manages to seem extremely conventional, at least to me, in his Western jeans and leather jacket.

He's busy taking notes and looks very concentrated. I've just taken a peep. Writing is my natural enemy, especially Chinese writing that manages to convey meaning without sound, and groups of entities rather than just one entity. But I couldn't resist. His notes are in Chinese ideograms, very nicely drawn too. No trouble with spelling here. I even think he might well stay here, if only for that reason. This is his first big journalistic experience, of something he can understand and can report on intelligibly. He would also have the backing of his father, who has suddenly become a national figure, and whatever they say, nepotism still functions here. And everywhere in fact. Perhaps he'll become a Chinese star-newscaster Han-yo Man-Ing?

But all this, all over the place, is only a beginning. Sport, Adventure, Opinion Polls, old films, historical assessments, public phone-ins, sociological problem programs, medical information, the lot, still have to get their slimming diets, not to mention Computer Networks, Telephone Networks, Air Travel, Space Satellites, Big Business, Small and Medium Business, Stock Exchanges, International Finance, Banking, Government, Administration... At this rate Hanjo will be an old man before Verbivore is resolved.

18

This is ridiculous. Clearly I'm still obsessed with Decibel. But it's totally unrealistic, how can she inform the alphaguys? She merely measures noise, she can't transmit content. It wouldn't be admitted even in science fiction, and alas, we're not living this as science fiction but as all too painful reality. I may hate noise, but I can't exist unless radio returns, so I'm as involved as anyone. I'll have to scratch all that. My novel isn't going at all well. And it's all complicated by the fact that Perry's back, and is writing a novel about Verbivore, with me as main character, stranded in Moscow and writing a novel about Verbivore.

All that information about the meetings is important, though, and if I'm stranded in Moscow how else could I know about it and present it convincingly? I'll have to find some other way, a real delegate-at-large, going everywhere. But it would take him months and months to get everywhere, whereas the meetings are occurring simultaneously. And will continue to do so for years. Yuri could talk to me about Dostoevski's notion of the invisible secretary, and perhaps from there have me appointed as delegate-at-large.

This Julian is nuts. How could the Russians appoint HIM? Sheer megalomania. Of course I'm no longer in Moscow but he is. And despite all my reading and research (chiefly in the press), I still know very little about Verbivore as a scientific phenomenon, especially from the Russian viewpoint, which was THE point. So I'm stuck with my novel as I was stuck in Moscow. And although I finally got out, it wasn't through any derringdo on my part but entirely thanks to the authorities, or Juri's kindness (or desire to get rid of me). And no authority or kindness is going to get me out of this mess, the mess of wordprocessing a novel, except my own authorial authority.

I can't even talk to Mira about it. I know she could help me, she really seemed to know about Verbivore. But she's moved right out of my ken. I can't ring, and she doesn't answer my letters. Fine Producer of Radio Drama, no concern for wordprocessors! It's true this isn't a radio play. In any case, I learnt from the desk downstairs, who put me through to her secretary, that she's now a Deputy Creative Director. Fat lot of use she is in deputy creation, I said, and she replied that this was the post Miss Enketei held for normal times, but that like everyone else, she's now engaged on Verbivore research. But that's exactly what I need, I said, I'm writing a novel about Verbivore. From a Russian viewpoint, I added to impress her. Well, she said, she's Director of Public Reaction Analysis at the moment, so I doubt whether she could help as to a Russian viewpoint. And she's far too busy to see you without an appointment. Why don't you write her a letter?

Well of course, I didn't like to admit I had sent her letters, several, so I said good idea, thank you, and went away disconsolate. I must continue to depend purely on the press, and on my imagination. Which is stretched to breaking point. And the press is more repetitive than the media ever were. Why aren't there creatures to penalise print into economy too? At least it would help save forests and prevent floods.

I know. I'll write a play instead. With Paula in the star role. She'll love that. People are flocking to the theatres. Then I can concentrate chiefly on "Public Reaction", analysed or not, well, analysed in my fashion. I'll do without Mira, without everyone. I'll concentrate on ordinary people, I've always been good at those. There's plenty of material in readers' letters. I could still transmute it all to Russia, and use my observations on the Russian people. A grand gin and vodka cocktail, human reactions are after all much the same everywhere, but the neorealistic Soviet element and the tragic Slav element will give it extra spice. A Turgenev type play, a twenty-first century Turgenev! That's it! Julian can be her son, or a young lover. Or the eternal student. Or an English student stranded in Moscow. Shall I ever get from Moscow? Or maybe I'll fuse him with Anatol. I'll have to see as I go. At last I'm on to something. I can do a play in a week, I'm an old hand, whereas novels take much longer. Not that plays are easier, they're extremely tricky, but the rhythm is faster, and the dialogue guides me, and tells me exactly when it's gone on too long and needs an entrance or other happening. A play is a quick-pace microcosm, whereas a novel is like organising a whole world in slow motion.

Come on then, old Hupsos the Sublime, type away. VERBIVORE, Act I, Scene 1. No. THE VERBIVORE WOMAN. That's it. People are themselves verbivore, and women most of all. That gives me a human angle.

> The new play at The Haymarket is a winner. The human angle on Verbivore.
> Perry Hupsos has come up with a superhit.
> Dame Paula in the role of the Verbivore Woman has surpassed herself.
> Very funny. Don't miss it!
> Deeply serious, moving, and dazzlingly witty at the same time.
> A domestic comedy on Verbivore. The insuperable challenge has been met by Perry Hupsos.
> A twenty-first century Turgenev.
> A twenty-first century Tchechov.
> An English Gogol.
> Paula James is a triumph.

Paula, congratulations, and thank you, thank you.
Perry darling! But without you –
Congrats, mum, you were a scream.
Zab, my love, what a lovely surprise! But why didn't you tell me you were coming? I'd have got you a free ticket.
I got one, mum, by saying I'm your daughter. They believed me, too! Couldn't let you know as I wasn't sure of getting here.
This is Perry Hupsos, the author. Without him –
You mean you're THE Zab, of Jip and Zab and Xorandor?
Well, yes.

Holy shit! Excuse me. I hope I didn't make too many howlers.

Howlers? Why no, though you made us howl with laughter. You cleverly avoided all the technical aspect and –

Paula! You were marvellous.

Tim darling! So we meet again at last.

I was in Australia. Back last week. Took ages. This is so refreshing, after all the meetings I've had to attend.

So, what's happening?

Oh, endless argy-bargy everywhere, many accepting cuts in principle but not in practice, others rebelling against blind and monstrous censorship. But we'll get there in the end.

But Tim, how will they KNOW? The creatures I mean.

We have no idea. But we must be ready.

Unto the day. Well I hope you're ready to come to the party, simply everyone will be there.

Where's Jip, mum?

He's been in Canada. But he promised to try and come over for the play, if he could get a sailing. Not easy these days, and he's already been on detachment from Nasa for simply ages, as he explained, so I fear – Jip! You made it!

Hi mum. You were superb. Very funny. And moving.

My pet, you're too kind. It was a challenge, with such an expert family to scrutinise me.

Nonsense, one must relax sometimes and this was real entertainment. Hi Zab. How's the euromping? Hi, Tim. May I see you tomorrow? I have an interim report from George as well as my own.

Now no shop, you two. You said relax and relax is what you're going to do. Where's the champagne? Here, waiter, bring that bubbly over, will you?

Congratulations, Dame Paula.

Oh, did you see it?

No ma'am, we were preparing the reception. But I've heard the first reviews are excellent. I intend to see it.

You shall get a ticket, I'll tell them, what is your name?

Thank you, Dame Paula. If you will permit, I'll go and write it down, you're so surrounded, and rightly so, you

might forget it. And I do want to see the play.
You do that thing. More champagne, everywhere. I believe the Prime Minister is coming.
Where's Mira?
Who's Mira, Tim? Don't say you've got a girlfriend at last?
She's my assistant. She came with me, but she seems to have eclipsed herself.
Well, I had a bit. As much as I love discussions among few, so much do I detest the roar of parties. I sound like Decibel, very selective as to types of noise. But also I didn't feel I belonged. I never do, in a way, and there I'm more like Zab. Ever since I had to give up Greek. I simulated belonging, as redundant teacher inventing terrorists in a tumbledown farm, as radio drama producer, as deputy creative director, as head of Public Reaction Analysis, as Tim's newly appointed assistant. Always going on as if.
The play is a genuine success. Perry's back in the limelight, as Perry Hupsos not Striker, that's all dropped. He's a bit drunk with it all, but why not? So is Paula. So are the whole cast. There are daily queues a mile long. Bookings full for months. It will be another Mousetrap, the longest run in history, and still running after seventy years. Or will it?

That last query must have been instinctive. It did run, for eight months, the last one to an emptier and emptier house, even though people had booked. For suddenly, six weeks ago, the waves opened up again. The technicians who'd been patiently trying to transmit for two years with test programs were caught napping. Nothing was ready. But they quickly recovered and went into action. All over the world the same thing happened. The press announced it half triumphantly, information oblige. Transistors were switched on, television sets lit up, telephones were tried, shyly and economically at first then interminably. Computer networks are zinging away again, international finance is out of its doldrums, satellites are working, the space stations are in communication again and at last replenished (just in time) by shuttle. Planes are flying again – though most airports took a week to get them into service and through security checks and their booking system working. It's business as usual, or rather, as before.

It seems that the television was the most missed, and zapping among local and world programs has become hysterical. It used to be only the couch-potatoes, retired or unemployed maniacs who spend ten hours a day zapping football matches all over the world, but now it's everyone: so many people were laid off that it's not easy to get the whole social machinery back into action again. Nobody goes to the theatre any more, nor to the bingohalls, the pinball alleys, the games halls, the gym halls, the sports stadiums, the innumerable emergency cinemas, the evening classes, nobody reads the newspapers, everyone is sitting at home, mesmerised by the forgotten small screen and the miraculous return of their favourite drug. I remember some early writer on mescaline experiences (the golden age of innocence!) explaining that there was no vacuum between images but a plenum of uninterrupted pulsations and oscillations. And the couch-potatoes used to talk of feeling the current pass into them, the magnetism.

The economy programs are accepted here, however, and in Germany, and generally in Europe, though France is more recalcitrant, and the Germans are going on about das Weltsystem being also ein Wertsystem, with Truth-Values. The States are thoroughly up in arms, and all the stations in the world who are furious about it are using their channels to discuss their problems, as if, though forced to obey out of fear, they wanted the alphaguys to understand how impossible it all is. In England, however, there's a generally game acceptance, and people are repeating in the press and in street interviews that nobody needs to be educated late at night with nature programs and intellectual debates, nobody needs to be bombarded with ads every few minutes (though most of their TV wouldn't exist without ads, and nor are they prepared to pay a higher licence fee for having no ads), nobody needs so many prize-winning games that merely rival each other in the same slots, nobody needs so many fictions. And so on. I wonder how long it will last, how soon the commercial pressures will start, the lobbies, the small expansions followed by bigger ones, the cheating. As is already happening elsewhere. In any case many countries hadn't come to any kind of agreement and weren't ready with tailored programs. Seems Uther has no sense of timing. But then, computers don't experience time as we do, they're merely databanks.

I'm busier than ever as Tim's assistant, and also keep a now distant eye on Public Reaction Analysis, though I have a deputy director. It's the same type analysis but a very different content, since the reactions are to the opposite phenomenon. But as predictable as ever, from "that'll show'm" to "Beware". However, the research is made much easier by the restored communication network.

But Tim's job has become almost untenable, and he's exhausted. He handed over his post as Managing Director and is now one of the International Controlers of Economy Programs. He has to fly off to Geneva all the time, to Moscow (yes, there is cooperation), to Montevideo, to Dakar, Cairo, Tokyo. He tries to snatch a few days' rest in each place, but it's difficult, everything is too urgent everywhere, and he's in permanent jetlag. He's also very depressed. Nobody is really observing the rules, even the stations which accepted them, and many are still indignantly refusing. All the arguments for economy are being turned on their heads. It won't apply to us, to our channel, famines and catastrophes are elsewhere. Death is for other cultures.

Man lives on simulations, he told me the other evening in a fit of discouragement over a drink at his flat. The media offer nothing but. What people don't realise is, so do computers, with their simulated world of computer viruses, computer decisions as to when different versions are required, say, in market research or on the stock exchange. Simulations a hundred times more sinister, because sillier and more powerful, than the old legends and myths and fictions.

I don't see why that's so terrible.

Not in itself. It's just that – how to put it without sounding a primitivist? Abstraction was early associated with secrecy, with a small but controlling priestly elite, with the art of writing, which slowly dematerialised the world, and printing accelerated this, into a condition of pure speed, pure mind. A sort of weightlessness, a flight. Well, this process has been multiplied a millionfold, at an ever-increasing speed, and today we live in a world that's totally materialistic at one level and totally immaterial and illusory at another.

But Tim, isn't it only a matter of degree? Mankind has always been materialistic and spiritual at the same time. And what you're saying is in itself abstract, a sort of flight.

But now we have one lot of abstract simulators threatening to silence the others. What shall we be left with?

I'm not sure whether he was aware of his own turn-around. I uttered soothing noises: But surely everyone will calm down, surely they've learnt their lesson during those two years of radio silence?

On the surface, perhaps. But passions remain. What if Verbivore returned, what if we failed the test? It would be for good this time, for ever. We endured it because we can endure anything if we know there may or even might be an end, a light at the end of the tunnel as politicians never tire of saying. But next time, knowing it's for ever, mankind will not endure it. It has become enslaved to immediate communication of every kind, for its wars, its terrorism, its pleasure, its understanding, for companionship in solitude. Eventually someone, some group, some nation, some alliance of countries, will let its passions run wild and express them through the ultimate violence, and destroy the planet.

Real or newsreel? I think you're being unduly pessimistic, Tim. Besides, what about the scientific solution Andrewski kept going on about? Doesn't technology always find a way to meet a new crisis, however slowly?

I don't see any kind of opening that way myself, but then, I'm no longer a specialist. And slowly's probably the right word. It would be a race against human horror.

If you mean nuclear horror that's become almost a quaint idea these days, and almost to be welcomed against the slow sick extinction from lack of ozone and other pollutions. Everyone knows it can't be used, hence official disarmament.

Everyone knows the real danger, besides pollution, is economic, and that the real enemy isn't a specific and basically European nation but the smooth anciently resentful orientals and Africans we humiliated in the past, whose revenge has been economic and merciless.

Precisely. Our institutions depended on performative utterances, in other words, sincerity of a sort, legal procedures and democratic processes generally. But we seem to be going back to primitive methods, hostages, terrorism, fanaticism, which had their point in the last colonial wars when even mighty powers like Russia or America had to withdraw, but today they go on, and sincerity and judgment now seem as outmoded as belief in trial by water or fire.

I think you overrate our sincerity, as you call it, and they, whoever that might be, have their own form of sincerity.

No doubt. But if the real enemy is economic, as you say, look at the almost total collapse of world economy during Verbivore. It would all start again, and with a vengeance, and for good.

But what about Zab's idea that these creatures need information as we need to breathe? Surely they would try us out again, in order to get it, but more orderly? Surely they would realise, after a while, that they opened up the waves before we were ready?

Perhaps. But I doubt it. Mankind cannot be orderly.

You're exhausted, Tim, give yourself a break.

Sorry. You're right. Let's have another drink and then I'll see you home.

You will not, you'll go straight to bed and have an early night, I'll get a taxi.

Okay, thanks, Mira. Here's yours for the road, then. Let's watch the news, it's ten.

– is the news. A Lufthansa plane has crashed as it was coming in to land in Munich, from Paris (images of broken fuselage among fir-trees). There are no survivors. The Prime Minister has left (images of P.M. climbing into plane and waving) for the Moscow International Summit on Broadcasting Economy Enforcement. Famine threatens in

Blank screen, black with millions of white dots, like a universe.

Decibel dies.

OHIO UNIVERSITY LIBRARY

Please return this book as soon as you have finished with it. In order to avoid a fine it must be returned by the latest date stamped below.